Teacher Resource Copymasters

HOUGHTON MIFFLIN

Math Steps

HOUGHTON MIFFLIN

Boston • Atlanta • Dallas • Denver • Geneva, Illinois • Palo Alto • Princeton

Contents

Assessments 1

The assessment copymasters give you valuable information about your students' prior knowledge, progress, and understanding of new mathematical content.

From the beginning of the year through the end of the year, you can assess students' understanding of mathematical skills, concepts, and vocabulary. Both free-response and multiple-choice tests are provided. The results of these tests can help you assess whether students have the necessary prerequisite skills and knowledge to be successful with this year's materials, whether students are progressing adequately, and whether students have achieved the goals of the mathematics curriculum.

Reteach Worksheets 67

Reteach Worksheets meet the needs of students who require reinforcement of topics or concepts. The step-by-step instruction on each worksheet supports students through the learning process. The Teacher Note at the bottom of each page tells you when to use the worksheet.

Reteach Worksheets support lessons in a unit. In the Student Book, there is a Quick Check feature that appears at the end of many lessons. The Quick Check reviews the lessons you have just covered. If students have difficulty with any of the concepts or skills on the Quick Check, they can use the Reteach Worksheets that correspond to the items. The references to Reteach Worksheets appear in the Teacher Edition in both the Annotated Student Book pages and in the Lesson Support.

Extension Worksheets

Extension Worksheets cover a variety of mathematical content. They give students an opportunity to extend a topic they are learning, or they introduce students to new topics.

The Extension Worksheets are organized by unit. The Teacher Note at the bottom of each page tells you when to use the worksheet. References to Extension Worksheets appear in the Teacher Edition.

Teaching Resources

Teaching Resources are copymasters for frequently used teaching aids and for Family Projects. You may use the teaching aids during the presentation of a lesson or an activity, or reproduce them for students to use individually. Family Projects provide suggestions for students and their families to work together on the skills and objectives in each unit.

Answer Keys

Answer Keys include answers for all of the assessments, as well as the Reteach Worksheets and Extension Worksheets.

Assessments

Assessment Overview

At the Beginning of the Year

• Beginning of the Year Inventory

Before your students start Unit 1, you may give them the Beginning of the Year Inventory. This pretest shows whether students possess the necessary prerequisite skills and knowledge to be successful with this year's mathematics. You can also use the Inventory as a placement test for students who transfer to your school during the school year. The Inventory uses free-response format to test objectives that cover skills, concepts, problem solving, and vocabulary.

Before Each Unit

• Unit Pretest

Assessing prior knowledge helps you build effective lessons using what students already know. You will quickly know which skills, concepts, and vocabulary your students need to review before they begin a new unit. By using the results of these tests, you can prepare your students to be confident and successful with the mathematics in the new unit.

During Each Unit

• Quick Checks in the Student Book

You can use Quick Checks to monitor and assess students' progress at regular intervals. Each Quick Check reviews the lessons you have just covered. References to the Reteach worksheets and Skills Tutorial appear in the Teacher Edition in both the Annotated Student Book and in the Lesson Support.

After Each Unit

• Unit Posttest

Each unit posttest is an additional tool you may use to assess students' mathematical understanding and application of the work in that unit. The posttests are formatted like the Unit Reviews in the Student Book and cover all unit objectives.

At Midyear

• Midyear Test

The Midyear Test covers objectives from Units 1 through 6 in the Student Book. Test results will show which skills or concepts you need to review with students. This test is in standardized format to provide your students with valuable experience in taking standardized tests.

At the End of the Year

• Final Test

The Final Test covers objectives from Units 7 through 12 in the Student Book, as well as emphasized objectives from each unit in the first half of the book. You can use this summative test to reinforce the topics taught throughout the year and to assess what students have mastered. The Final Test is in standardized format to provide your students with more test-taking practice.

Write the sum.

1.

3 + 2 = _____

2.

1¢ + 3¢ = _____ ¢

Write the difference. Write how many fewer.

3.

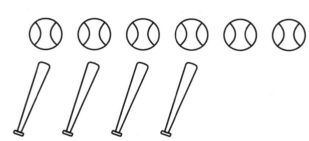

6 − 4 = _____

_____ fewer bats

Write the difference. Write how many more.

4.

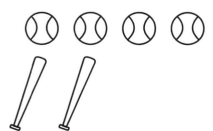

4 − 2 = _____

_____ more balls

Cross out to subtract.

5.

4 − 3 = _____

6.

6¢ − 3¢ = _____ ¢

Look at the picture. Write the addition or subtraction fact.

7.

____ ◯ ____ = ____

8.

____ ◯ ____ = ____

Complete the fact family.

9.

3 + 2 = ☐

____ + ____ = ☐

____ − ____ = ☐

____ − ____ = ☐

10.

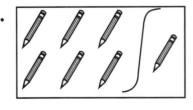

6 + 1 = ☐

____ + ____ = ☐

____ − ____ = ☐

____ − ____ = ☐

Write how many tens and ones.
Write the number.

11.

_____ tens _____ ones = _____

12.

_____ tens _____ ones = _____

Write the number.

13. What number is between
10 and 12?

_____

14. What number is just
after 11?

_____

Ring the number that is greater.

15. 27   32

16. 74   47

Look at the picture.
Ring the seventh flower.

17.

first

Write the missing numbers.

18. 23, 24, _____, _____

19. 19, _____, 17, _____

Add or subtract.

20.   2
      + 2
      _____

21.   6
      − 3
      _____

22.   3
      + 1
      _____

23.   5
      − 2
      _____

Write the missing number.

24. $8 + \underline{} = 10$

25. $6 + \underline{} = 9$

Ring the correct answer.

26. What day of the week is just after Monday?

Sunday   Tuesday   Saturday

27. What day of the week is just before Saturday?

Friday   Tuesday   Monday

Add or subtract.

28. $3 + 6 = \underline{}$

29. $10 − 1 = \underline{}$

Write the time.

30.

 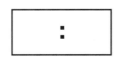

31.

 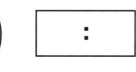

Add or subtract.

32.
```
   3
   2
 + 1
```

33.
```
   4
   1
 + 5
```

34.
```
   7
   1
 + 0
```

35.
```
   5
   1
 + 2
```

36.
```
   4
 + 2
```

37.
```
  10
 - 3
```

38.
```
   7
 - 2
```

39.
```
   4
 + 4
```

40.
```
  44
 + 2
```

41.
```
  53
 - 1
```

42.
```
  29
 + 10
```

43.
```
  78
 - 3
```

Write the total.

44.

_____ ¢

45.

_____ ¢

Skip-count by 2's.

46.

14, _____ , _____ , 20, _____ , 24

Solve.

47. Color one fourth.

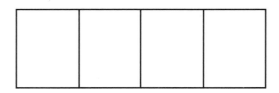

48. Color one third.

Ring which shows equal parts.

49.

 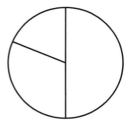

Ring the longer pencil.

50.

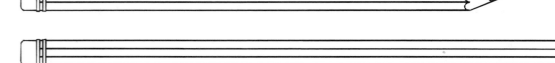

Solve.

51. Ring the flower next to the tree.
Ring the bird above the flower.

Ring the correct answer.

52. What is the name?

triangle   square   rectangle

53. What is the name?

cylinder   cube   cone

54. How many sides?

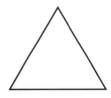

two   three   four

55. How many corners?

three   four   five

Draw what comes next.

56.

Write the number sentence.

57. Jan has 3 cats. Luis has 4 cats.
How many cats do they have in all?

____ ⃝ ____ = ____

Draw a picture. Write the answer.

58. Kim has 8 balloons. 2 fly away.
Juan has 5 balloons. Who has
more balloons?

_____

Look for a pattern. Complete the table to solve.

59. There are 4 children. Each child
has 5 crayons. How many crayons
do the 4 children have in all?

_____ crayons

children	1	2	3	4	5
crayons	5	10			

Read the graph. Answer the questions.

60.

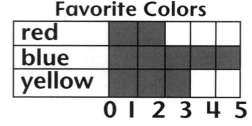

Favorite Colors

How many children like yellow?

_____ children

How many more children like

blue than red? _____ children

Guess the amount. Can you buy the item?
Ring yes or no.

61.

yes   no

Complete. Then, write a related addition or subtraction fact. (1A)

1. $6 + 3 = \boxed{}$ | **2.** $11 - 2 = \boxed{}$ | **3.** $4 + 3 = \boxed{}$

_____ | _____ | _____

Complete the fact family. (1A)

4. $\begin{array}{r} 4 \\ + 5 \\ \hline \end{array}$ $+ \underline{} \quad - \underline{} \quad - \underline{}$

5. $\begin{array}{r} 1 \\ + 5 \\ \hline \end{array}$ $+ \underline{} \quad - \underline{} \quad - \underline{}$

6. $\begin{array}{r} 3 \\ + 9 \\ \hline \end{array}$ $+ \underline{} \quad - \underline{} \quad - \underline{}$

7. $\begin{array}{r} 4 \\ + 6 \\ \hline \end{array}$ $+ \underline{} \quad - \underline{} \quad - \underline{}$

Solve. (1A)

8. $\begin{array}{r} 2 \\ + 7 \\ \hline \end{array}$ **9.** $\begin{array}{r} 7 \\ + 3 \\ \hline \end{array}$ **10.** $\begin{array}{r} 4 \\ + 4 \\ \hline \end{array}$ **11.** $\begin{array}{r} 9 \\ + 4 \\ \hline \end{array}$ **12.** $\begin{array}{r} 6 \\ + 5 \\ \hline \end{array}$ **13.** $\begin{array}{r} 2 \\ + 8 \\ \hline \end{array}$ **14.** $\begin{array}{r} 3 \\ + 5 \\ \hline \end{array}$

15. $\begin{array}{r} 12 \\ - 6 \\ \hline \end{array}$ **16.** $\begin{array}{r} 9 \\ - 7 \\ \hline \end{array}$ **17.** $\begin{array}{r} 8 \\ - 6 \\ \hline \end{array}$ **18.** $\begin{array}{r} 13 \\ - 5 \\ \hline \end{array}$ **19.** $\begin{array}{r} 10 \\ - 7 \\ \hline \end{array}$ **20.** $\begin{array}{r} 9 \\ - 2 \\ \hline \end{array}$ **21.** $\begin{array}{r} 12 \\ - 5 \\ \hline \end{array}$

Solve. (1B)

22.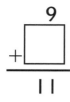

23.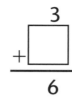

24.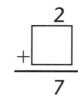

25.

Use >, <, or =. (1C)

26. 12 ◯ 5

27. 6 ◯ 11

28. 14 ◯ 14

29. 3 + 2 ◯ 9 − 8

30. 11 ◯ 4 + 9

31. 6 ◯ 9 + 1

Add. (1D)

32.
```
   2
   3
 + 1
```

33.
```
   1
   4
 + 3
```

34.
```
   4
   6
 + 4
```

35.
```
   6
   2
 + 4
```

Problem Solving Reasoning ## Solve. (1E)

36. Jenny has **4** crayons. She gets **8** more crayons. How many crayons does she have in all?

_____ ◯ _____ = _____

_____ crayons

37. Leo has **14** marbles. He gives **7** of them to his friend. How many marbles does he have left?

_____ ◯ _____ = _____

_____ marbles

Complete. Then, write a related addition or subtraction fact. (1A)

1. $4 + 2 =$ ☐

_____

2. $12 - 3 =$ ☐

_____

3. $6 + 7 =$ ☐

_____

Complete the fact family. (1A)

4.
$$
\begin{array}{r} 9 \\ + 2 \end{array} \quad + \underline{} \quad - \underline{} \quad - \underline{}
$$

5.
$$
\begin{array}{r} 3 \\ + 5 \end{array} \quad + \underline{} \quad - \underline{} \quad - \underline{}
$$

6.
$$
\begin{array}{r} 4 \\ + 8 \end{array} \quad + \underline{} \quad - \underline{} \quad - \underline{}
$$

7.
$$
\begin{array}{r} 6 \\ + 3 \end{array} \quad + \underline{} \quad - \underline{} \quad - \underline{}
$$

Solve. (1A)

8.	9.	10.	11.	12.	13.	14.
$\begin{array}{r} 1 \\ + 9 \end{array}$	$\begin{array}{r} 7 \\ + 5 \end{array}$	$\begin{array}{r} 4 \\ + 7 \end{array}$	$\begin{array}{r} 8 \\ + 2 \end{array}$	$\begin{array}{r} 6 \\ + 8 \end{array}$	$\begin{array}{r} 2 \\ + 6 \end{array}$	$\begin{array}{r} 3 \\ + 8 \end{array}$

15.	16.	17.	18.	19.	20.	21.
$\begin{array}{r} 11 \\ - 5 \end{array}$	$\begin{array}{r} 9 \\ - 4 \end{array}$	$\begin{array}{r} 12 \\ - 6 \end{array}$	$\begin{array}{r} 13 \\ - 8 \end{array}$	$\begin{array}{r} 9 \\ - 7 \end{array}$	$\begin{array}{r} 10 \\ - 2 \end{array}$	$\begin{array}{r} 11 \\ - 3 \end{array}$

Solve. (1B)

22.
```
    8
 +□
 ───
   12
```

23.
```
    4
 +□
 ───
   10
```

24.
```
    7
 +□
 ───
    9
```

25.
```
    6
 +□
 ───
   10
```

Use >, <, or =. (1C)

26. 10 ◯ 12

27. 13 ◯ 5

28. 8 ◯ 8

29. 4 + 2 ◯ 9 − 8

30. 13 ◯ 4 + 9

31. 7 ◯ 9 + 4

Add. (1D)

32.
```
   3
   3
 + 4
 ───
```

33.
```
   5
   1
 + 3
 ───
```

34.
```
   2
   5
 + 4
 ───
```

35.
```
   3
   6
 + 4
 ───
```

Problem Solving Reasoning Solve. (1E)

36. Dean colors **5** pictures. Then, he colors **8** more. How many pictures does he color in all?

_____ ◯ _____ = _____

_____ pictures

37. Tasha finds **9** seashells. She gives **5** seashells to her brother. How many seashells does she have left?

_____ ◯ _____ = _____

_____ shells

Unit 2 Pretest

Complete. (2B)

1.

_____ tens and _____ ones = _____

forty-three

2.

_____ tens and _____ ones = _____

sixty-seven

Use >, <, or =. (2A)

3. 28 ◯ 35

4. 64 ◯ 47

5. 39 ◯ 21

6. 56 ◯ 56

7. 27¢ ◯ 72¢

8. 61¢ ◯ 16¢

9. 56¢ ◯ 86¢

10. 68¢ ◯ 8¢

Ring the greatest number. (2A)

11.   69   96   91

Ring the least number. (2A)

12.   16   42   62

What comes (2A)

| before? | Between? | After? |

13. _____, 17

14. _____, 36

15. 14, _____, 16

16. 11, _____, 13

17. 18, _____

18. 20, _____

Complete. (2B)

19.

	Tens	Ones
47		
18		
25		

20.

Tens	Ones	
8	4	
5	1	
9	3	

Complete. (2D)

21. 4 tens and 5 ones = ☐ + ☐ = ☐

22. 7 tens and 2 ones = ☐ + ☐ = ☐

Count by 2's. (2C)

23.

12	14				24			

Count by 5's. (2C)

24.

5	10			35			

Match. (2E)

25. 5 dimes and 6 pennies   71¢

26. 7 dimes and 1 penny   56¢

27. 1 dime and 7 pennies   17¢

Problem Solving Reasoning | **How many are there? Guess then check.**

28.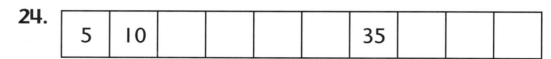

guess _____   check _____

Complete. (2B)

1.

_____ tens and _____ ones = _____

thirty-two

2.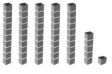

_____ tens and _____ ones = _____

fifty-six

Use >, <, or =. (2A)

3. 36 ◯ 22

4. 41 ◯ 50

5. 57 ◯ 78

6. 82 ◯ 82

7. 16¢ ◯ 60¢

8. 52¢ ◯ 52¢

9. 43¢ ◯ 78¢

10. 66¢ ◯ 9¢

Ring the greatest number. (2A)

11.   39   96   31

Ring the least number. (2A)

12.   47   77   44

What comes (2A)

| before? | Between? | After? |

13. _____, 15

14. _____, 32

15. 9, _____, 11

16. 15, _____, 17

17. 14, _____

18. 19, _____

Complete. (2B)

19.

	Tens	Ones
36		
58		
29		

20.

Tens	Ones	
7	5	
5	3	
6	8	

Complete. (2D)

21. 3 tens and 7 ones = ☐ + ☐ = ☐

22. 8 tens and 0 ones = ☐ + ☐ = ☐

Count by 3's. (2C)

23.

3		9				21			

Count by 10's. (2C)

24.

10					60				

Match. (2E)

25. 4 dimes and 9 pennies   68¢

26. 6 dimes and 8 pennies   19¢

27. 1 dime and 9 pennies   49¢

Problem Solving Reasoning

How many are there?
Guess then check.

28.

guess _____   check _____

Complete. Then, write a related addition or subtraction fact. (3A)

1. $9 + 7 =$ ☐

_____

2. $13 - 6 =$ ☐

_____

3. $17 - 8 =$ ☐

_____

Write the fact family. (3A)

4.   5, 9, 14

+_____ +_____ −_____ −_____

5.   7, 8, 15

+_____ +_____ −_____ −_____

6.   8, 8, 16

+_____ −_____

7.   8, 9, 17

+_____ +_____ −_____ −_____

Solve. (3B)

8. $6 +$ ☐ $= 12$

9. $8 +$ ☐ $= 14$

10. $3 +$ ☐ $= 11$

11.
```
    9
 +☐
 ────
   18
```

12.
```
    7
 +☐
 ────
   16
```

13.
```
    7
 +☐
 ────
   14
```

14.
```
    8
 +☐
 ────
   13
```

Use + or −. (3B)

15. ◯ 8
       8
     ___
      16

16. ◯ 15
        8
     ___
       7

17. ◯ 7
       3
     ___
      10

18. ◯ 12
        5
     ___
       7

Use >, <, or =. (3A)

19. 15 ◯ 12

20. 3 + 6 ◯ 11

21. 4 + 4 ◯ 8

22. 2 + 7 ◯ 17

23. 14 − 5 ◯ 11

24. 15 ◯ 8 + 6

Add. (3C)

25.   5
       3
     + 5
     ___

26.   6
       4
     + 7
     ___

27.   3
       7
     + 4
     ___

28.   6
       5
     + 6
     ___

Problem Solving Reasoning **Write the number sentence. Solve.** (3D)

29. Betty has **6** red balls, **3** yellow balls, and **8** green balls. How many balls does she have in all?

____ ____ ____  ____

_____ balls

30. There are **13** kittens in all. **8** of the kittens have spots. How many kittens do not have spots?

____ ____ ◯ ____

_____ kittens

Complete. Then, write a related addition or subtraction fact. (3A)

1. 18 − 9 = ☐

_____

2. 12 − 5 = ☐

_____

3. 9 + 6 = ☐

_____

Write the fact family. (3A)

4.   6, 9, 15

___ + ___ ___ + ___ ___ − ___ ___ − ___

5.   7, 9, 16

___ + ___ ___ + ___ ___ − ___ ___ − ___

6.   6, 8, 14

___ + ___ ___ + ___ ___ − ___ ___ − ___

7.   9, 8, 17

___ + ___ ___ + ___ ___ − ___ ___ − ___

Solve. (3B)

8. 7 + ☐ = 12

9. 9 + ☐ = 15

10. 7 + ☐ = 14

11.
$$\begin{array}{r} 9 \\ + \boxed{} \\ \hline 17 \end{array}$$

12.
$$\begin{array}{r} 8 \\ + \boxed{} \\ \hline 16 \end{array}$$

13.
$$\begin{array}{r} 7 \\ + \boxed{} \\ \hline 15 \end{array}$$

14.
$$\begin{array}{r} 5 \\ + \boxed{} \\ \hline 12 \end{array}$$

Use + or −. (3B)

15.   ◯ 9
         9
       ‾‾‾‾
        18

16.   ◯ 14
         6
       ‾‾‾‾
         8

17.   ◯ 7
         4
       ‾‾‾‾
        11

18.   ◯ 12
         9
       ‾‾‾‾
         3

Use >, <, or =. (3A)

19. 4 ◯ 14

20. 7 + 7 ◯ 14

21. 4 + 8 ◯ 11

22. 8 + 7 ◯ 17

23. 14 ◯ 9 + 5

24. 16 − 7 ◯ 9

Add. (3C)

25.   6
       4
     + 6
     ‾‾‾‾

26.   8
       4
     + 3
     ‾‾‾‾

27.   7
       7
     + 4
     ‾‾‾‾

28.   4
       5
     + 6
     ‾‾‾‾

Problem Solving Reasoning **Write the number sentence. Solve.** (3D)

29. Bobby has **5** red pencils, **6** yellow pencils, and **2** green pencils. How many pencils does he have in all?

 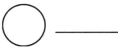 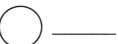

_____ pencils

30. Ali picks **16** flowers. **9** of the flowers are red. How many are not red?

 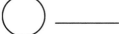

_____ flowers

Match. (4A)

1. sphere

2. cone

3. cube

Look at the solids.
Complete the table. (4A)

Solid	Number of flat faces	Stacks	Rolls
4.			
5.			
6.			

Write how many sides and corners. (4A)

7.

_____ sides

_____ corners

8.

_____ sides

_____ corners

9.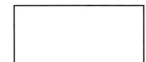

_____ sides

_____ corners

Ring the figure that is congruent to the first figure. (4A)

10.

Color one part.
Ring the correct fraction. (4B)

11.

$\dfrac{1}{5}$ $\dfrac{1}{6}$

12.

$\dfrac{1}{10}$ $\dfrac{1}{8}$

13.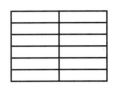

$\dfrac{1}{12}$ $\dfrac{1}{10}$

14.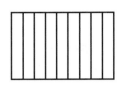

$\dfrac{1}{9}$ $\dfrac{1}{8}$

Ring the fraction that shows what part is colored. (4B)

15.

$\dfrac{1}{4}$ $\dfrac{2}{5}$ $\dfrac{1}{6}$

16.

$\dfrac{1}{3}$ $\dfrac{2}{3}$ $\dfrac{3}{4}$

17.

$\dfrac{1}{2}$ $\dfrac{4}{5}$ $\dfrac{5}{6}$

18.

$\dfrac{1}{8}$ $\dfrac{1}{9}$ $\dfrac{1}{10}$

Ring $\dfrac{1}{4}$ of each set. (4C)

19.

$\dfrac{1}{4}$ of 12 = _____

20.

$\dfrac{1}{4}$ of 8 = _____

Use the picture to solve. (4D)

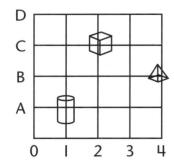

21. Where is the cylinder? _____

22. Where is the cube? _____

23. Where is the
square pyramid? _____

Match. (4A)

1. sphere

2. rectangular prism

3. cylinder

Look at the solids.
Complete the table. (4A)

Solid	Number of flat faces	Stacks	Rolls
4. 			
5.			
6.			

Write how many sides and corners. (4A)

7.

_____ sides

_____ corners

8.

_____ sides

_____ corners

9.

_____ sides

_____ corners

Ring the figure that is congruent to the first figure. (4A)

10.

Color one part.
Ring the correct fraction. (4B)

11.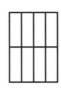

$\frac{1}{5}$ $\frac{1}{8}$

12.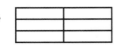

$\frac{1}{6}$ $\frac{1}{8}$

13.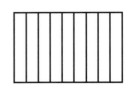

$\frac{1}{8}$ $\frac{1}{9}$

14.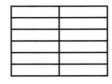

$\frac{1}{12}$ $\frac{1}{10}$

Ring the fraction that shows what part is colored. (4B)

15.

$\frac{1}{3}$ $\frac{2}{5}$ $\frac{4}{5}$

16.

$\frac{1}{4}$ $\frac{2}{3}$ $\frac{3}{6}$

17.

$\frac{3}{4}$ $\frac{3}{5}$ $\frac{5}{6}$

18.

$\frac{4}{5}$ $\frac{3}{6}$ $\frac{4}{10}$

Ring $\frac{3}{4}$ of each set. (4C)

19.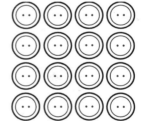

$\frac{3}{4}$ of 16 = _____

20.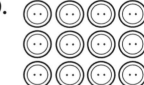

$\frac{3}{4}$ of 12 = _____

Use the picture to solve. (4D)

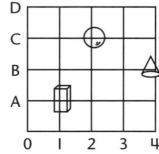

21. Where is the cone? _____

22. Where is the sphere? _____

23. Where is the rectangular prism? _____

Measure with a centimeter ruler. (5A)

1.

about _____ centimeters

2.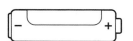

about _____ centimeters

Measure with an inch ruler. (5A)

3.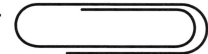

about _____ inches

4.

about _____ inches

Ring the words that tell about the object. (5B)

5.

| less than a pound | about a pound | more than a pound |

6.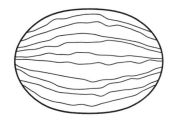

| less than a pound | about a pound | more than a pound |

7.

| less than a kilogram | about a kilogram | more than a kilogram |

8.

| less than a kilogram | about a kilogram | more than a kilogram |

How far has each caterpillar gone? (5A)

9. about ⬜ inches

10. about ⬜ inches

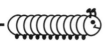

Read each Fahrenheit thermometer. (5C)

11.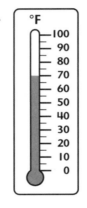

_____ degrees

12.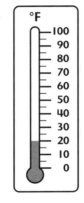

_____ degrees

13.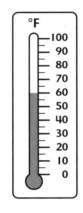

_____ degrees

Problem Solving / Reasoning **Use an inch ruler, then write a number sentence to solve.** (5D)

14. What is the length of the path?

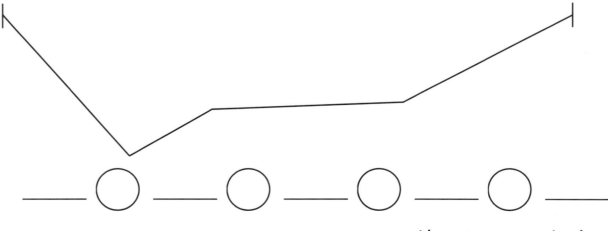

About _____ inches

Measure with a centimeter ruler. (5A)

1.

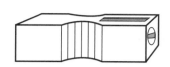

about _____ centimeters

2.

about _____ centimeters

Measure with an inch ruler. (5A)

3.

about _____ inches

4.

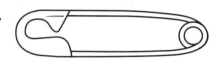

about _____ inches

Ring the words that tell about the object. (5B)

5.

| less than a pound | about a pound | more than a pound |

6.

| less than a pound | about a pound | more than a pound |

7.

| less than a kilogram | about a kilogram | more than a kilogram |

8.

| less than a kilogram | about a kilogram | more than a kilogram |

Name _____

How far has each grasshopper gone? (5A)

9. about ☐ inches

---

10. about ☐ inches

Read each Fahrenheit thermometer. (5C)

11.

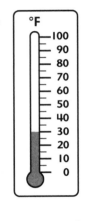

_____ degrees

12.

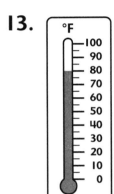

_____ degrees

13.

_____ degrees

Problem Solving
Reasoning

Use an inch ruler, then write a number sentence to solve. (5D)

14. What is the length of the path?

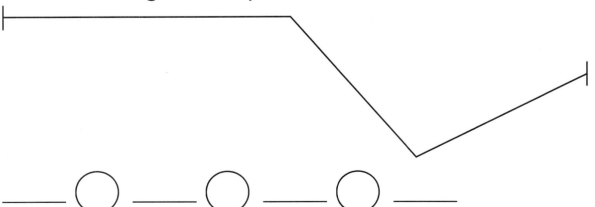

About _____ inches

Add. (6A)

1. 3 tens + 2 tens = _____ tens

    30 + 20 = _____

2. 2 tens + 5 tens = _____ tens

    20 + 50 = _____

3. 20 + 25 = _____

4. 45 + 30 = _____

Add. (6B)

5. $\begin{array}{r} 32 \\ + 15 \\ \hline \end{array}$

6. $\begin{array}{r} 18 \\ + 27 \\ \hline \end{array}$

7. $\begin{array}{r} 45 \\ + 24 \\ \hline \end{array}$

8. $\begin{array}{r} 23 \\ + 60 \\ \hline \end{array}$

9. $\begin{array}{r} 37 \\ + 16 \\ \hline \end{array}$

10. $\begin{array}{r} 14¢ \\ + 54¢ \\ \hline \end{array}$

11. $\begin{array}{r} 41 \\ + 23 \\ \hline \end{array}$

12. $\begin{array}{r} 67¢ \\ + 15¢ \\ \hline \end{array}$

13. $\begin{array}{r} 37 \\ + 42 \\ \hline \end{array}$

14. $\begin{array}{r} 21 \\ + 45 \\ \hline \end{array}$

15. $\begin{array}{r} 55 \\ + 22 \\ \hline \end{array}$

16. $\begin{array}{r} 19 \\ + 49 \\ \hline \end{array}$

17. $\begin{array}{r} 14 \\ 23 \\ + 13 \\ \hline \end{array}$

18. $\begin{array}{r} 21 \\ 35 \\ + 31 \\ \hline \end{array}$

19. $\begin{array}{r} 51 \\ 11 \\ + 14 \\ \hline \end{array}$

20. $\begin{array}{r} 36 \\ 15 \\ + 10 \\ \hline \end{array}$

21. $\begin{array}{r} 43 \\ 32 \\ + 13 \\ \hline \end{array}$

22. $\begin{array}{r} 16 \\ 18 \\ + 52 \\ \hline \end{array}$

Problem Solving Reasoning **Solve the problems that have enough information.**
(6C)

23. There are **62** purple grapes. There are **16** white grapes. How many green grapes are there?

    Answer: _____

24. There are **14** yellow bananas. There are **38** green bananas. How many bananas are there in all?

    Answer: _____

Add. (6A)

1. 2 tens + 6 tens = _____ tens

    20 + 60 = _____

2. 3 tens + 4 tens = _____ tens

    30 + 40 = _____

3. 15 + 25 = _____

4. 30 + 55 = _____

Add. (6B)

5.   13
  + 54

6.   33
  + 28

7.   49
  + 17

8.   35¢
  + 25¢

9.   68
  + 13

10.   22
  + 57

11.   47
  + 26

12.   58¢
  + 14¢

13.   34
  + 48

14.   56
  + 24

15.   66
  + 13

16.   18
  + 71

17.   24
    18
  + 11

18.   32
    23
  + 35

19.   42
    13
  + 15

20.   12
    53
  + 24

21.   15
    15
  + 29

22.   19
    34
  + 24

Problem Solving Reasoning	**Solve the problems that have enough information.**

(6C)

23. There are **53** orange buttons. There are **16** red marbles. How many blue blocks are there?

Answer: _____

24. There are **43** red ribbons. There are **27** blue ribbons. How many ribbons are there in all?

Answer: _____

Subtract. (7A)

1. 7 tens − 2 tens = _____ tens

70 − 20 = _____

2. 6 tens − 3 tens = _____ tens

60 − 30 = _____

3. 65 − 35 = _____

4. 85 − 40 = _____

Subtract. (7B)

5. 42
− 15

6. 76
− 37

7. 55
− 14

8. 63¢
− 30¢

9. 37
− 9

10. 54
− 34

11. 82
− 29

12. 67¢
− 45¢

13. 57
− 8

14. 26
− 15

15. 75
− 24

16. 43
− 41

17. 42
− 29

18. 37
− 14

19. 85
− 59

20. 92
− 27

21. 47¢
− 22¢

22. 55
− 36

| Problem Solving Reasoning | **Use the table. Solve.** (7C) |

23. How many flowers did James and Ming pick in all on Saturday?

_____ flowers

Flowers Picked		
	Saturday	Sunday
James	37	22
Ming	29	41

24. How many more flowers did Ming pick on Sunday than on Saturday?

_____ more flowers

Subtract. (7A)

1. 5 tens − 4 tens = _____ ten

50 − 40 = _____

2. 7 tens − 4 tens = _____ tens

70 − 40 = _____

3. 75 − 40 = _____

4. 65 − 20 = _____

Subtract. (7B)

5.
53
− 26

6.
65
− 26

7.
77¢
− 27¢

8.
43
− 20

9.
48
− 9

10.
72
− 44

11.
71
− 29

12.
53
− 35

13.
69
− 18

14.
34
− 15

15.
62¢
− 51¢

16.
49
− 19

17.
38
− 19

18.
47¢
− 22¢

19.
58
− 31

20.
93
− 48

21.
56
− 35

22.
62
− 36

Problem Solving Reasoning **Use the table. Solve.** (7C)

Seashells Found		
	Day 1	Day 2
Jamal	23	34
Dion	38	42

23. How many more seashells did Dion find than Jamal on Day 1?

_____ more seashells

24. How many seashells did Jamal and Dion find in all on Day 2?

_____ seashells

Show the time on the clock. (8B)

1.

10:15

2.

3:35

3.

9:55

4.

6:05

Fill in the blank. (8B)

5. There are _____ minutes in 1 hour.

6. There are 7 days in _____ week.

7. There are 24 _____ in 1 day.

8. There are _____ months in 1 year.

Show the time on the clock. Solve. (8C)

9. Beth read her book from

_____ P.M.   _____ P.M.

She read for _____ minutes.

10. Shannon watched a movie from

_____ P.M.   _____ P.M.

She watched the movie

for _____ hours.

How much money? (8D)

11.  _____ ¢

12.  _____ ¢

13.  _____ ¢

Ring enough money. (8D)

14.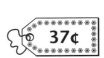

15.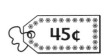

Use >, <, or =. Solve. (8E)

16. 4 dimes = _____ ¢   6 nickels = _____ ¢

4 dimes ◯ 6 nickels

17. 2 quarters = _____ ¢   5 dimes = _____ ¢

2 quarters ◯ 5 dimes

Problem Solving Reasoning **Make a list to solve.** (8F)

18. How many different ways can you make 25¢, using only

nickels and dimes? _____

_____

Show the time on the clock. (8B)

1.

4:20

2.

8:40

3.

12:10

4.

7:55

Fill in the blank. (8B)

5. There are 60 minutes in _____ hour.

6. There are _____ days in 1 week.

7. There are _____ hours in 1 day.

8. There are 12 months in 1 _____ .

Show the time on the clock. Solve. (8C)

9. Maney walked his dog from

_____ P.M.   _____ P.M.

He walked the dog for

_____ minutes.

10. Dixie played soccer from

_____ P.M.   _____ P.M.

She played soccer for

_____ hours.

How much money? (8D)

11.

_____ ¢

12.

_____ ¢

13.

_____ ¢

Ring enough money. (8D)

14.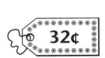

15.

Use >, <, or =. Solve. (8E)

16. **5** dimes = _____ ¢   **7** nickels = _____ ¢

5 dimes $\bigcirc$ 7 nickels

17. **I** quarter = _____ ¢   **4** dimes = _____ ¢

I quarter $\bigcirc$ 4 dimes

Problem Solving Reasoning **Make a list to solve.** (8F)

18. How many different ways can you make 35¢, using only

nickels and dimes? _____

_____

Use the tally chart to complete the graph. Solve. (9A)

1. **Favorite Pets in Grade 2**

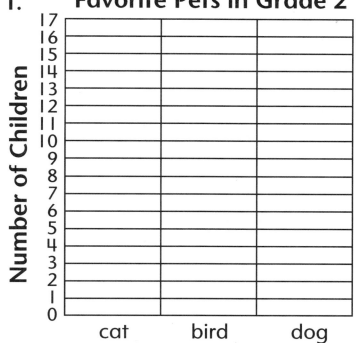

cat	‖‖‖ ‖‖‖ ‖
bird	‖‖‖ ‖‖‖
dog	‖‖‖ ‖‖‖ ‖‖‖ ‖

2. How many children like

cats the best? _____

3. Which pet has the least

votes? _____

Ring your prediction. (9B)

4. Will you sometimes, always, or never pick a white button from the bag? (9B)

sometimes   always   never

5. Are you more likely or less likely to land on gray? (9B)

more likely

less likely

Use the graph. Choose + or − to solve. (9C)

Books Read

	0	1	2	3	4	5	6	7	8	9	10
Jeff											
Tia											
Lou											

6. How many more books did Lou read than Tia?

_____ ◯ _____ = _____

_____ more books

Use the tally chart to complete the graph. Solve. (9A)

1.

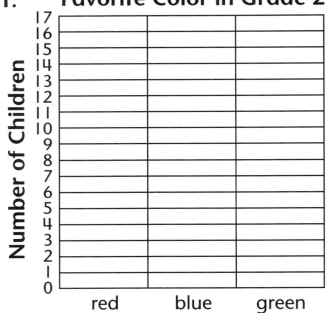

Favorite Color in Grade 2

Number of Children

17 16 15 14 13 12 11 10 9 8 7 6 5 4 3 2 1 0

red   blue   green

red	卌 卌			
blue	卌				
green	卌 卌 卌		

2. How many children like

blue the best? _____

3. Which color has the most

votes? _____

Ring your prediction. (9B)

4. Will you sometimes, always, or never pick a black marble from the bag? (9B)

sometimes   always   never

5. Are you more likely or less likely to land on gray? (9B)

more likely

less likely

Use the graph. Choose + or − to solve. (9C)

Games Won

Lynn										
Paul										
Ian										

0   1   2   3   4   5   6   7   8   9   10

6. How many more games did Paul win than Ian?

_____ ◯ _____ = _____

_____ more games

What comes (10A)

before?	Between?	After?
1. _____, 340	2. 529, _____, 531	3. 419, _____

Ring the greatest number. (10A)

4. 367   673   637

Ring the least number. (10A)

5. 771   781   718

Complete. (10B)

6. 209 is ____ hundreds ____ tens ____ ones.

7. 668 is ____ hundreds ____ tens ____ ones.

Complete. (10C)

8. 400 + 70 + 1 = [ ]

9. 500 + 40 + 3 = [ ]

10. 700 + 7   = [ ]

11. 900 + 60 + 0 = [ ]

Write the amount in two ways. (10D)

12.   _____ ¢

$._____

13.    _____ ¢

$._____

Problem Solving Reasoning **Use the picture. Solve.** (10E)

14.

Which costs more, the cat or the dog?

_____ ◯ _____

The _____ costs more.

What comes (10A)

before?	Between?	After?
1. _____, 290	2. 619, _____, 621	3. 680, _____

Ring the greatest number. (10A) | Ring the least number. (10A)

4. 641   614   416 | 5. 389   398   893

Complete. (10B)

6. 772 is ____ hundreds ____ tens ____ ones.

7. 506 is ____ hundreds ____ tens ____ ones.

Complete. (10C)

8. 900 + 7 = [ ]   10. 600 + 30 + 0 = [ ]

9. 400 + 80 + 2 = [ ]   11. 800 + 10 + 9 = [ ]

Write the amount in two ways. (10D)

12.  _____ ¢

$. _____

13.  _____ ¢

$. _____

Use the picture. Solve. (10E)

14.

Which costs more, the bird or the duck?

_____ ◯ _____

The _____ costs more.

Add or subtract. (11A)

1.	378	2.	438	3.	630	4.	167	5.	559
	+ 214		− 129		− 209		+ 527		− 217

6.	674	7.	329	8.	782	9.	248	10.	695
	+ 325		+ 256		− 313		+ 347		− 166

11.	115	12.	951	13.	470	14.	861	15.	372
	+ 467		− 227		+ 318		− 605		+ 518

Add or subtract. Use $. (11B)

16.	$1.75	17.	$6.37	18.	$4.36	19.	$8.28	20.	$5.50
	+ 2.05		− 1.28		+ 2.18		− 6.15		− 1.25

Problem Solving Reasoning **Solve.** (11C)

21. Debbie bought a pen for $2.87 and a notebook for $1.09. How much money did she spend?

Answer: _____

22. Lee has 7 dollars, 2 quarters, 2 dimes, 1 nickel, and 3 pennies. How much change does he have after he buys a game for $5.30?

Answer: _____

Add or subtract. (11A)

| 1. | 295 | 2. | 615 | 3. | 345 | 4. | 148 | 5. | 839 |
| | − 157 | | − 409 | | + 328 | | + 515 | | − 625 |

| 6. | 752 | 7. | 578 | 8. | 943 | 9. | 412 | 10. | 668 |
| | + 129 | | − 169 | | − 215 | | + 278 | | − 539 |

| 11. | 125 | 12. | 857 | 13. | 515 | 14. | 776 | 15. | 285 |
| | + 666 | | − 345 | | + 149 | | − 307 | | + 308 |

Add or subtract. Use $. (11B)

| 16. | $2.65 | 17. | $7.28 | 18. | $4.37 | 19. | $9.75 | 20. | $5.67 |
| | + 1.15 | | − 2.09 | | + 2.46 | | − 7.39 | | − 1.19 |

Problem Solving Reasoning **Solve.** (11C)

21. Leroy bought a sandwich for $3.49 and juice for $1.28. How much money did he spend?

22. Joyce has 5 dollars, 3 quarters, 1 dime, 2 nickels, and 2 pennies. How much does she have left after she buys lunch for $3.20?

Answer: _____

Answer: _____

Skip-count to find the total. (12A)

1.   ____ groups of ____

____, ____, ____, ____, ____   ____ in all

2.   ____ groups of ____

____, ____, ____, ____   ____ in all

3.   ____ groups of ____

____, ____, ____   ____ in all

Find the product. (12A)

4. $\begin{array}{r} 2 \\ \times\, 4 \\ \hline \end{array}$

5. $\begin{array}{r} 6 \\ \times\, 3 \\ \hline \end{array}$

Find the product. (12B)

6. $\begin{array}{r} 7 \\ \times\, 2 \\ \hline \end{array}$
7. $\begin{array}{r} 4 \\ \times\, 3 \\ \hline \end{array}$
8. $\begin{array}{r} 3 \\ \times\, 5 \\ \hline \end{array}$
9. $\begin{array}{r} 2 \\ \times\, 2 \\ \hline \end{array}$
10. $\begin{array}{r} 10 \\ \times\, 5 \\ \hline \end{array}$
11. $\begin{array}{r} 2 \\ \times\, 6 \\ \hline \end{array}$

12. $\begin{array}{r} 8 \\ \times\, 3 \\ \hline \end{array}$
13. $\begin{array}{r} 10 \\ \times\, 2 \\ \hline \end{array}$
14. $\begin{array}{r} 2 \\ \times\, 5 \\ \hline \end{array}$
15. $\begin{array}{r} 0 \\ \times\, 2 \\ \hline \end{array}$
16. $\begin{array}{r} 3 \\ \times\, 6 \\ \hline \end{array}$
17. $\begin{array}{r} 5 \\ \times\, 5 \\ \hline \end{array}$

18. $\begin{array}{r} 10 \\ \times\, 6 \\ \hline \end{array}$
19. $\begin{array}{r} 4 \\ \times\, 5 \\ \hline \end{array}$
20. $\begin{array}{r} 3 \\ \times\, 7 \\ \hline \end{array}$
21. $\begin{array}{r} 10 \\ \times\, 9 \\ \hline \end{array}$
22. $\begin{array}{r} 3 \\ \times\, 3 \\ \hline \end{array}$
23. $\begin{array}{r} 2 \\ \times\, 4 \\ \hline \end{array}$

Ring equal groups.
Write the number in each group. (12C)

24.

6 is 2 groups of _____.

25.

15 is 3 groups of _____.

26.

12 is 4 groups of _____.

27.

10 is 5 groups of _____.

28.

4 is 2 groups of _____.

29.

20 is 4 groups of _____.

Problem Solving Reasoning

Choose the operation.
Write a number sentence. Solve. (12D)

30. One duck has **2** legs.
How many legs are on **8** ducks? _____

add   subtract   multiply   _____ legs

Skip-count to find the total. (12A)

1.

_____ groups of _____

_____, _____, _____   _____ in all

2.

_____ groups of _____

_____, _____, _____, _____, _____   _____ in all

3.

_____ groups of _____

_____, _____, _____, _____   _____ in all

Find the product. (12A)

4.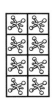

$$\begin{array}{r} 2 \\ \times\,4 \\ \hline \end{array}$$

5.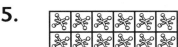

$$\begin{array}{r} 6 \\ \times\,2 \\ \hline \end{array}$$

Find the product. (12B)

6. $\begin{array}{r} 5 \\ \times\,2 \\ \hline \end{array}$
7. $\begin{array}{r} 2 \\ \times\,3 \\ \hline \end{array}$
8. $\begin{array}{r} 3 \\ \times\,4 \\ \hline \end{array}$
9. $\begin{array}{r} 10 \\ \times\,3 \\ \hline \end{array}$
10. $\begin{array}{r} 2 \\ \times\,7 \\ \hline \end{array}$
11. $\begin{array}{r} 3 \\ \times\,9 \\ \hline \end{array}$

12. $\begin{array}{r} 8 \\ \times\,2 \\ \hline \end{array}$
13. $\begin{array}{r} 10 \\ \times\,4 \\ \hline \end{array}$
14. $\begin{array}{r} 2 \\ \times\,9 \\ \hline \end{array}$
15. $\begin{array}{r} 3 \\ \times\,1 \\ \hline \end{array}$
16. $\begin{array}{r} 10 \\ \times\,0 \\ \hline \end{array}$
17. $\begin{array}{r} 4 \\ \times\,5 \\ \hline \end{array}$

18. $\begin{array}{r} 2 \\ \times\,2 \\ \hline \end{array}$
19. $\begin{array}{r} 3 \\ \times\,5 \\ \hline \end{array}$
20. $\begin{array}{r} 0 \\ \times\,6 \\ \hline \end{array}$
21. $\begin{array}{r} 6 \\ \times\,2 \\ \hline \end{array}$
22. $\begin{array}{r} 4 \\ \times\,6 \\ \hline \end{array}$
23. $\begin{array}{r} 10 \\ \times\,8 \\ \hline \end{array}$

Ring equal groups.
Write the number in each group. (12C)

24.

9 is 3 groups of _____.

25.

20 is 4 groups of _____.

26.

10 is 2 groups of _____.

27.

15 is 5 groups of _____.

28.

8 is 2 groups of _____.

29.

12 is 4 groups of _____.

Problem Solving Reasoning

Choose the operation.
Write a number sentence. Solve. (12D)

30. One spider has 8 legs.
How many legs are on 2 spiders? _____

add   subtract   multiply   _____ legs

Midyear Test
Pages 51–56

Item Analysis

Items	Unit Obj.
1	1A
2	1E
3	2A
4	2B
5, 6	2C
7	2D
8	2E
9	2F
10, 28	3A
11	3D
12, 13	4A
14, 15	4B
16, 17	4C
18	4D
19, 20	5A
21	5B
22	5C
23	5D
24	6C
25	1B
26	1C
27	1D
29	3B
30	3C
31	6A
32	6B

Answers to Midyear Test items can be found on page 256.

Administering the Test

These pages review concepts and skills from the unit as well as providing practice with standardized test formats. Children should fill in the circle for the correct answer.

Test-Taking Tip Remind children to listen carefully to the entire problem before choosing their answer.

Exercises 1–24 The first 24 items of the test are administered orally. Before reading each exercise, ask children to find the correct item number and then listen carefully. Read each exercise twice, and pause between items to give children time to find and mark their answers.

ex. 1. *Which number sentence belongs to this fact family?*

ex. 2. *Joe has 6 hats. Anya has 7 hats. How many hats do they have in all?*

ex. 3. *Mark the number that is between 59 and 61.*

ex. 4. *Look at the number 93. What number is in the tens place?*

ex. 5. *Look at the number pattern. Which number most likely comes next?*

ex. 6. *There is a missing number in the pattern. Mark under the number that should go in the empty box.*

ex. 7. *Mark under the number that shows 6 tens and 8 ones.*

ex. 8. *How many dimes are in 58¢?*

ex. 9. *Which number sentence describes how many butterflies were seen on Wednesday and Thursday?*

ex. 10. *Look at the number sentence 7 + 9 = 16. Mark the related fact.*

ex. 11. *Jenna has 15 stuffed animals. She has 7 bears. How many are not bears? Mark the number sentence that shows how many of her stuffed animals are not bears.*

ex. 12. *Mark the one that has 2 flat faces.*

ex. 13. *Mark the figure with 5 corners.*

ex. 14. *What fraction of this figure is shaded?*

ex. 15. *Mark the fraction that shows which part is shaded.*

ex. 16. *What fraction of the circles are white?*

ex. 17. *Mark under the box that shows 1/2 of 12 balls shaded.*

ex. 18. *Where is the triangle?*

ex. 19. *Use your inch ruler to measure the path from point A to point C.*

ex. 20. *Use your centimeter ruler to measure from the tree to the bench. How many centimeters is it from the tree to the bench?*

ex. 21. *Mark under the object that weighs more than a pound.*

ex. 22. *Mark the thermometer that shows 30 degrees.*

ex. 23. *Jesse has a bag with 5 pounds of apples. Manuel has a bag with 12 pounds of apples. How much heavier is Manuel's bag of apples?*

ex. 24. *Saleem has 64 tickets. He can get two items. Which two items will equal exactly 64 tickets? Mark your answer.*

Exercises 25–32 Tell the class that they will complete exercises 25–32 of the Midyear Test independently.

Test-Taking Tip Remind children that NH stands for Not Here, meaning that the correct answer to the problem is not one of the answer choices given.

After the Test

The Item Analysis chart on page 49 shows the unit objective covered by each test item. This chart can help you determine which objectives need review or extra practice.

1

6, 8, 14

○ $6 + 6 = 12$ ○ $14 - 8 = 6$

○ $8 + 5 = 13$ ○ $14 - 7 = 7$

2

 **6**   **7**

1	5	8	13
○	○	○	○

3

59		61

50	58	60	62
○	○	○	○

4

93

3	6	9	12
○	○	○	○

5

20, 25, 30, 35, ▢

30	36	40	45
○	○	○	○

6

48		52	54

46	49	50	51
○	○	○	○

7

6 tens and 8 ones	63	67	68	86
	○	○	○	○

8

5 dimes	6 dimes	7 dimes	8 dimes
○	○	○	○

9

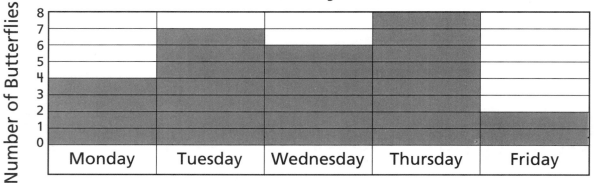

Butterfly Count

$4 + 7 = 11$	$7 + 6 = 13$	$7 + 2 = 9$	$6 + 8 = 14$
○	○	○	○

10

$7 + 9 = 16$

○ $16 - 9 = 7$ ○ $9 + 5 = 14$
○ $8 + 7 = 15$ ○ $16 - 8 = 8$

11

○ $15 - 5 = 10$ ○ $15 - 7 = 8$
○ $9 + 6 = 15$ ○ $15 + 7 = 22$

12

   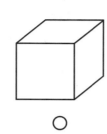   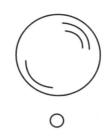   

○   ○   ○   ○

13

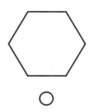   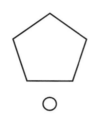      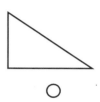

○   ○   ○   ○

14

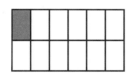

$\dfrac{1}{4}$ $\dfrac{1}{6}$ $\dfrac{2}{10}$ $\dfrac{1}{12}$

○   ○   ○   ○

15

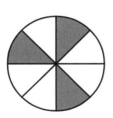

$\dfrac{5}{3}$ $\dfrac{3}{5}$ $\dfrac{3}{8}$ $\dfrac{5}{8}$

○   ○   ○   ○

16

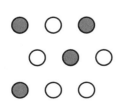

$\dfrac{5}{4}$ $\dfrac{4}{5}$ $\dfrac{4}{9}$ $\dfrac{5}{9}$

○   ○   ○   ○

17

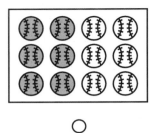

○   ○   ○   ○

18

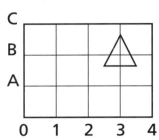

3, B   3, C   2, C   B, 4

○   ○   ○   ○

19

1 inch   3 inches   4 inches   5 inches

○   ○   ○   ○

20

4 centimeters   7 centimeters   10 centimeters   12 centimeters

○   ○   ○   ○

21

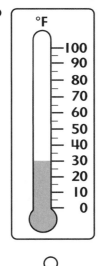

　○　　　　　　○　　　　　　○　　　　　　○

22

| °F | °F | °F | °F |

○　　　　　　　○　　　　　　　○　　　　　　　○

23

5 pounds　　　7 pounds　　　12 pounds　　　17 pounds

○　　　　　　　○　　　　　　　○　　　　　　　○

24

  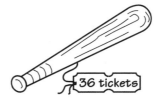 

41 tickets　　　28 tickets　　　36 tickets　　　40 tickets

| 41 | , | 28 |　　| 41 | , | 36 |　　| 28 | , | 40 |　　| 28 | , | 36 |

○　　　　　　　○　　　　　　　○　　　　　　　○

25

$\boxed{} + 5 = 12$

5	7	8	17	NH
○	○	○	○	○

26

$14 \bigcirc 7$

+	−	>	<	NH
○	○	○	○	○

27

$$\begin{array}{r} 3 \\ 5 \\ +\ 6 \\ \hline \end{array}$$

8	9	12	15	NH
○	○	○	○	○

28

$17 - 9 = \boxed{}$

12	8	5	2	NH
○	○	○	○	○

29

$9 + \boxed{} = 18$

11	10	9	0	NH
○	○	○	○	○

30

$8 + 8 + 2 = \boxed{}$

12	15	16	17	NH
○	○	○	○	○

31

$30 + 37 = \boxed{}$

63	67	68	70	NH
○	○	○	○	○

32

$$\begin{array}{r} 47 \\ +\ 28 \\ \hline \end{array}$$

60	64	70	71	NH
○	○	○	○	○

Final Test
Pages 59–66

Item Analysis

Items	Unit Obj.
1	2A
2	4B
3	5A
4	6A
5	7C
6	8A
7	8B
8	8C
9	8D
10	8E
11, 12	8F
13, 14	9A
15	9B
16	9C
17	10A
18	10B
19	10C
20	10D
21	10E
22	11C
23	12A
24	12C
25	12D
26	1A
27	3B
28, 29	6B
30, 31	7A
32, 33	7B
34, 35	11A
36, 37	11B
38, 39	12B

Answers to Final Test items can be found on page 256.

Administering the Test

These pages review concepts and skills from the unit as well as providing practice with standardized test formats. Children should fill in the circle for the correct answer.

Test-Taking Tip Remind children to listen carefully to the entire problem before choosing their answer.

Exercises 1–25 The first 25 items of the test are administered orally. Before reading each exercise, ask children to find the correct item number and then listen carefully. Read each exercise twice, and pause between items to give children time to find and mark their answers.

ex. 1. Which of these numbers is greater than 40 and less than 70?

ex. 2. Which picture shows one fourth of a circle?

ex. 3. Use your inch ruler to measure the length of this pencil. About how many inches long is it?

ex. 4. Michelle has 30 stickers. Soha has 40 stickers. How many stickers do the two girls have in all?

ex. 5. Which shows a reasonable estimate for the problem?

ex. 6. Which clock shows 8:55?

ex. 7. Which digital clock shows the same time as the analog clock?

ex. 8. The first clock shows when Walter left to go to the park. The second clock shows when Walter got back. How long was Walter at the park?

ex. 9. Look at the collection of coins. What is the value?

ex. 10. Look at the four collections of coins. Which collection of coins is worth the least?

ex. 11. Look at Sam's schedule. Where will Sam go just after lunch?

ex. 12. What time does school end?

ex. 13. Look at the picture graph. How many more books did Liz read than Joey?

ex. 14. How many books did Carlo and Joey read altogether?

ex. 15. Which type of marble are you most likely to pull out of this bag?

ex. 16. Which of these number sentences would be made true if you put a subtraction sign in the circle?

ex. 17. Which number is ten more than 786?

ex. 18. Which number shows 3 hundreds, 7 tens, and 4 ones?

ex. 19. Which shows the same as 947?

ex. 20. What is the value of the collection of coins?

ex. 21. How many pencils can 5 boxes hold? Use the table. Look for a pattern to solve the problem.

ex. 22. Which shows a reasonable estimate for the answer?

ex. 23. Sara planted 4 rows of cabbages with 4 cabbages in each row. Which number sentence tells how many cabbages she planted in all?

ex. 24. The teacher has 12 marbles. She wants to give each child 2 marbles. How many children can she give two marbles to?

ex. 25. Choose the picture that shows the following problem: Steve has 4 plates. He puts 5 strawberries on each plate. How many strawberries does he have in all?

Exercises 26–39 Tell the class that they will complete exercises 26–39 of the Final Test independently.

Test-Taking Tip Remind children that NH stands for Not Here, meaning that the correct answer to the problem is not one of the answer choices given.

After the Test
The Item Analysis chart on page 57 shows the unit objective covered by each test item. This chart can help you determine which objectives need review or extra practice.

Assessments

1

28	36	57	82
○	○	○	○

2

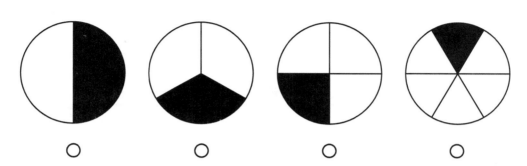

| ○ | ○ | ○ | ○ |

3

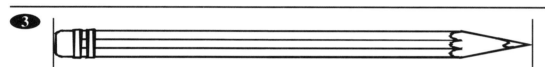

3 inches	4 inches	5 inches	6 inches
○	○	○	○

4

50	70	80	90
○	○	○	○

5

$$79 - 32$$

69 − 32 37	80 − 12 68	70 − 30 40	80 − 30 50
○	○	○	○

6

8:55

○　　　　○　　　　○　　　　○

7

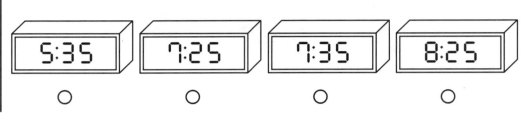

5:35　　　7:25　　　7:35　　　8:25

○　　　　○　　　　○　　　　○

8

○ 2 hours　　　　　　○ 3 hours

○ 3 hours 30 minutes　　○ 4 hours

9

42¢　　　46¢　　　47¢　　　57¢

○　　　　○　　　　○　　　　○

10

○

○

○

○

Sam's Schedule	
8:30	catch bus
9:00	school starts
10:30	recess
12:15	lunch
1:00	art class
3:00	school ends

11

○ recess   ○ soccer practice

○ art class   ○ home

12

○ 8:30   ○ 9:00   ○ 3:00   ○ 3:30

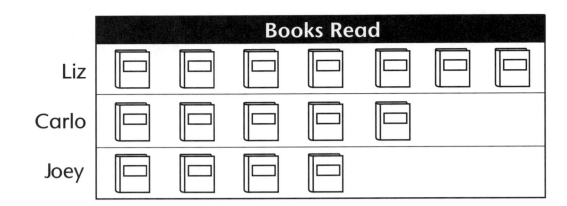

Books Read

Liz

Carlo

Joey

13

| 3 | 4 | 5 | 7 |
| ○ | ○ | ○ | ○ |

14

| 4 | 5 | 7 | 9 |
| ○ | ○ | ○ | ○ |

15

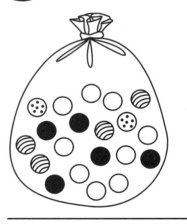

○   ○   ○   ○

16

○ 4 ○ 9 = 13   ○ 9 ○ 6 = 15

○ 20 ○ 10 = 10   ○ 7 ○ 5 = 12

17

786 | 787 789 796 886
         ○   ○   ○   ○

18

347 374 437 734
 ○   ○   ○   ○

19

947 | ○ 900 + 400 + 7   ○ 90 + 40 + 7

○ 900 + 70 + 4   ○ 900 + 40 + 7

20

○ $1.27   ○ 1.27¢

○ $1.32   ○ $142

21

60   80   90   100
○   ○   ○   ○

Number of boxes	1	2	3	4	5
Number of pencils	20	40	60		

22

$$\begin{array}{r} 128 \\ -\ 29 \\ \hline \end{array}$$

70   80   90   100
○   ○   ○   ○

23

○ 4 + 4 = 8   ○ 4 × 4 = 16

○ 4 + 4 + 4 = 12   ○ 4 × 2 = 8

24

2   4   6   8
○   ○   ○   ○

25

○

○

○

○

26

$$8 + 3 = \square$$

9	10	11	12	NH
○	○	○	○	○

27

$$16 - \square = 7$$

10	9	8	7	NH
○	○	○	○	○

28

$$\begin{array}{r} 47 \\ + 29 \\ \hline \end{array}$$

16	71	76	84	NH
○	○	○	○	○

29

$$\begin{array}{r} 11 \\ 24 \\ + 37 \\ \hline \end{array}$$

51	52	62	71	NH
○	○	○	○	○

30

$$\begin{array}{r} 75 \\ - 25 \\ \hline \end{array}$$

25	40	50	60	NH
○	○	○	○	○

31

$$\begin{array}{r} 94 \\ - 30 \\ \hline \end{array}$$

74	64	60	54	NH
○	○	○	○	○

32

$$84$$
$$- 53$$

41   39   31   29   NH
○   ○   ○   ○   ○

33

$$66$$
$$- 19$$

47   57   75   85   NH
○   ○   ○   ○   ○

34

$$257$$
$$+ 434$$

615   691   719   729   NH
○   ○   ○   ○   ○

35

$$767$$
$$- 439$$

236   336   338   396   NH
○   ○   ○   ○   ○

36

$$\$4.81$$
$$- .72$$

○ $3.01

○ $3.74

○ $4.78

○ $5.08

○ NH

37

$$\$4.37$$
$$+ 3.44$$

○ $7.01

○ $7.11

○ $7.81

○ $8.21

○ NH

38

$$5 \times 6 = \square$$

11   20   30   40   NH
○   ○   ○   ○   ○

39

$$10 \times 7 = \square$$

3   17   35   70   NH
○   ○   ○   ○   ○

Reteach Worksheets

NOTES

Name _____

Problem: 4 + 2 = ☐

2 + 4 = ☐

 4 + 2 = ☐

2 + 4 = ☐

 4 + 2 = ☐

2 + 4 = ☐

4 + 2 = 6

2 + 4 = 6

Complete.

1. 6 + 2 = ☐

2 + 6 = ☐

2. 7 + 1 = ☐

1 + 7 = ☐

3. 5 + 2 = ☐

____ + 5 = ☐

4. 4 + 3 = ☐

____ + 4 = ☐

5. 7 + 3 = ☐

____ + ____ = ☐

6. 5 + 0 = ☐

____ + ____ = ☐

Extra Support You may need to explain to children that in the sample problem, each number is shown by squares. If they add the squares, they will find the total number of squares in all.

Teacher Note: Use after Quick Check page 8 to reteach Unit 1, Lesson 1. (2)

Name _____

Problem:
$$\begin{array}{r} 3 \\ + 4 \\ \hline 7 \end{array} \qquad \begin{array}{r} 7 \\ - 4 \\ \hline \end{array}$$

$$\begin{array}{r} 3 \\ + 4 \\ \hline 7 \end{array} \qquad \begin{array}{r} 7 \\ - 4 \\ \hline 3 \end{array} \qquad \begin{array}{r} 3 \\ + 4 \\ \hline 7 \end{array} \Big/ \begin{array}{r} 7 \\ - 4 \\ \hline 3 \end{array}$$

Complete.

1.
$$\begin{array}{r} 3 \\ + 6 \\ \hline \boxed{9} \end{array} \Big/ \begin{array}{r} \boxed{9} \\ - 6 \\ \hline \boxed{3} \end{array}$$

2.
$$\begin{array}{r} 5 \\ + 1 \\ \hline \square \end{array} \qquad \begin{array}{r} \square \\ - 1 \\ \hline \square \end{array}$$

3.
$$\begin{array}{r} 3 \\ + 5 \\ \hline \square \end{array} \qquad \begin{array}{r} \square \\ - 5 \\ \hline \square \end{array}$$

4.
$$\begin{array}{r} 10 \\ - 1 \\ \hline \square \end{array} \qquad \begin{array}{r} \square \\ + 1 \\ \hline \square \end{array}$$

5.
$$\begin{array}{r} 9 \\ - 5 \\ \hline \square \end{array} \qquad \begin{array}{r} \square \\ + 5 \\ \hline \square \end{array}$$

6.
$$\begin{array}{r} 6 \\ - 2 \\ \hline \square \end{array} \qquad \begin{array}{r} \square \\ + 2 \\ \hline \square \end{array}$$

Extra Support You may need to have children model each problem with counters. Then, have them write the related facts.

Teacher Note: Use after Quick Check page 8 to reteach Unit 1, Lesson 2. **(2)**

Addition Facts

$$\begin{array}{r} 5 \\ +\ 2 \\ \hline 7 \end{array}$$

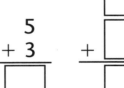

$$\begin{array}{r} 2 \\ +\ 5 \\ \hline 7 \end{array}$$

Subtraction Facts

$$\begin{array}{r} 7 \\ -\ 5 \\ \hline 2 \end{array}$$

$$\begin{array}{r} 7 \\ -\ 2 \\ \hline 5 \end{array}$$

Complete the fact family.

1. $2 + 4 = 6$

$4 + 2 = \boxed{6}$

$6 - 4 = \boxed{2}$

$6 - 2 = \boxed{4}$

2. $4 + 6 = \boxed{}$

$6 + 4 = \boxed{}$

$10 - 6 = \boxed{}$

$10 - 4 = \boxed{}$

3. $3 + 1 = \boxed{}$

$1 + 3 = \boxed{}$

$4 - 1 = \boxed{}$

$4 - 3 = \boxed{}$

4.
$$\begin{array}{r} 7 \\ +\ 3 \\ \hline \boxed{} \end{array} \qquad \begin{array}{r} \boxed{} \\ +\ \boxed{} \\ \hline \boxed{} \end{array}$$

$$\begin{array}{r} \boxed{} \\ -\ \\ \hline \boxed{} \end{array} \qquad \begin{array}{r} \boxed{} \\ -\ \\ \hline \boxed{} \end{array}$$

5.
$$\begin{array}{r} 5 \\ +\ 3 \\ \hline \boxed{} \end{array} \qquad \begin{array}{r} \boxed{} \\ +\ \boxed{} \\ \hline \boxed{} \end{array}$$

$$\begin{array}{r} \boxed{} \\ -\ \\ \hline \boxed{} \end{array} \qquad \begin{array}{r} \boxed{} \\ -\ \\ \hline \boxed{} \end{array}$$

6.
$$\begin{array}{r} 1 \\ +\ 7 \\ \hline \boxed{} \end{array} \qquad \begin{array}{r} \boxed{} \\ +\ \boxed{} \\ \hline \boxed{} \end{array}$$

$$\begin{array}{r} \boxed{} \\ -\ \\ \hline \boxed{} \end{array} \qquad \begin{array}{r} \boxed{} \\ -\ \\ \hline \boxed{} \end{array}$$

Extra Support You may need to have children model each fact as they complete the fact family.

Teacher Note: Use after Quick Check page 8 to reteach Unit 1, Lesson 3. **(2)**

Problem: $5 + \boxed{} = 8$

Look at the whole. What is the missing part?

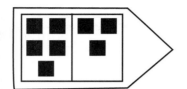

$5 + \boxed{} = 8$

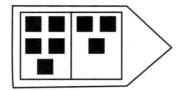

$5 + \boxed{3} = 8$

$5 + \boxed{3} = 8$

Complete.

1. $5 + \boxed{4} = 9$

2. $3 + \boxed{} = 4$

3. $6 + \boxed{} = 8$

4. $2 + \boxed{} = 7$

5. $7 + \boxed{} = 10$

6. $1 + \boxed{} = 6$

7.
$$\begin{array}{r} 3 \\ + \boxed{} \\ \hline 5 \end{array}$$

8.
$$\begin{array}{r} 5 \\ + \boxed{} \\ \hline 10 \end{array}$$

9.
$$\begin{array}{r} 7 \\ + \boxed{} \\ \hline 8 \end{array}$$

10.
$$\begin{array}{r} 4 \\ + \boxed{} \\ \hline 7 \end{array}$$

11.
$$\begin{array}{r} 9 \\ + \boxed{} \\ \hline 9 \end{array}$$

12.
$$\begin{array}{r} 8 \\ + \boxed{} \\ \hline 9 \end{array}$$

Extra Support Children may need support in modeling the addition. Guide them as they identify which is the part and which is the whole.

Teacher Note: Use after Quick Check page 16 to reteach Unit 1, Lesson 4. **(2)**

Problem: 6   13
           + 7   − 7
           ‾‾‾‾   ‾‾‾‾
            13

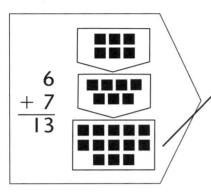

6   13
+ 7   − 7
‾‾‾   ‾‾‾
13   6

6   13
+ 7   − 7
‾‾‾   ‾‾‾
13   6

Complete.

1.   6   11
        + 5   − 5
        ‾‾‾‾   ‾‾‾‾
         11   6

2.   8   ☐
        + 5   − 5
        ‾‾‾‾   ‾‾‾‾
         13   ☐

3.   6   12
        + 6   − 6
        ‾‾‾‾   ‾‾‾‾
         ☐   ☐

4.   14   ☐
        − 5   + 5
        ‾‾‾‾   ‾‾‾‾
         ☐   ☐

5.   11   ☐
        − 7   + 7
        ‾‾‾‾   ‾‾‾‾
         ☐   ☐

6.   12   ☐
        − 8   + 8
        ‾‾‾‾   ‾‾‾‾
         ☐   ☐

Extra Support You may need to have children model each problem with counters. Then, have them write the related facts.

Teacher Note: Use after Quick Check page 16 to reteach Unit 1, Lesson 6. **(2)**   **73**

Addition Facts

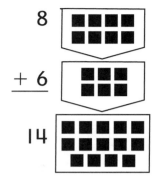

$$\begin{array}{r} 8 \\ + 6 \\ \hline 14 \end{array}$$

$$\begin{array}{r} 6 \\ + 8 \\ \hline 14 \end{array}$$

Subtraction Facts

$$\begin{array}{r} 14 \\ - 8 \\ \hline 6 \end{array}$$

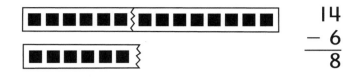

$$\begin{array}{r} 14 \\ - 6 \\ \hline 8 \end{array}$$

Complete the fact family.

1. $9 + 2 = 11$

$2 + 9 = \boxed{11}$

$11 - 2 = \boxed{9}$

$11 - 9 = \boxed{2}$

2. $8 + 5 = \boxed{}$

$5 + 8 = \boxed{}$

$13 - 5 = \boxed{}$

$13 - 8 = \boxed{}$

3. $5 + 7 = \boxed{}$

$7 + 5 = \boxed{}$

$12 - 7 = \boxed{}$

$12 - 5 = \boxed{}$

4.

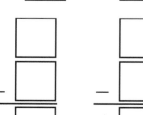

$$\begin{array}{r} 8 \\ + 4 \\ \hline \end{array} \qquad \begin{array}{r} \\ + \\ \hline \end{array}$$

$$\begin{array}{r} \\ - \\ \hline \end{array} \qquad \begin{array}{r} \\ - \\ \hline \end{array}$$

5.

$$\begin{array}{r} 9 \\ + 5 \\ \hline \end{array} \qquad \begin{array}{r} \\ + \\ \hline \end{array}$$

$$\begin{array}{r} \\ - \\ \hline \end{array} \qquad \begin{array}{r} \\ - \\ \hline \end{array}$$

6.

$$\begin{array}{r} 3 \\ + 8 \\ \hline \end{array} \qquad \begin{array}{r} \\ + \\ \hline \end{array}$$

$$\begin{array}{r} \\ - \\ \hline \end{array} \qquad \begin{array}{r} \\ - \\ \hline \end{array}$$

Extra Support You may need to have children model each fact as they complete the fact family.

Teacher Note: Use after Quick Check page 16 to reteach Unit 1, Lesson 7. **(2)**

You can group and add in any order.

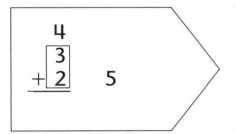

$$
\begin{array}{c}
4 \\
3 \\
+\ 2 \\
\hline
\end{array}
\quad 7
$$

$$
\begin{array}{c}
4 \\
3 \\
+\ 2 \\
\hline
\end{array}
\quad
\begin{array}{c}
7 \\
+\ 2 \\
\hline
9
\end{array}
$$

$$
\begin{array}{c}
4 \\
3 \\
+\ 2 \\
\hline
9
\end{array}
$$

$$
\begin{array}{c}
4 \\
3 \\
+\ 2 \\
\hline
\end{array}
\quad 5
$$

$$
\begin{array}{c}
4 \\
3 \\
+\ 2 \\
\hline
\end{array}
\quad
\begin{array}{c}
4 \\
+\ 5 \\
\hline
9
\end{array}
$$

Complete.

1.

$$
\begin{array}{c}
6 \\
4 \\
+\ 2 \\
\hline
\ \square\
\end{array}
\qquad
\begin{array}{c}
6 \\
+\ \boxed{6} \\
\hline
\boxed{12}
\end{array}
\qquad\qquad
\begin{array}{c}
6 \\
4 \\
+\ 2 \\
\hline
\ \square\
\end{array}
\qquad
\begin{array}{c}
\boxed{10} \\
+\ 2 \\
\hline
\boxed{12}
\end{array}
$$

2.

$$
\begin{array}{c}
7 \\
1 \\
+\ 6 \\
\hline
\ \square\
\end{array}
\qquad
\begin{array}{c}
\square \\
+\ 6 \\
\hline
\ \square\
\end{array}
\qquad\qquad
\begin{array}{c}
7 \\
1 \\
+\ 6 \\
\hline
\ \square\
\end{array}
\qquad
\begin{array}{c}
7 \\
+\ \square \\
\hline
\ \square\
\end{array}
$$

3. $(2 + 6) + 3 = \square$

4. $(5 + 5) + 3 = \square$

5. $2 + (2 + 8) = \square$

6. $6 + (3 + 3) = \square$

Extra Support Children may need to model and record the addition at each step. As children become more proficient, encourage them to use mental math strategies, such as making tens or doubling, to help them choose numbers to group when adding.

Teacher Note: Use after Quick Check page 22 to reteach Unit 1, Lesson 8. **(2)**

Reteach Worksheets

Use patterns to help remember names for numbers.

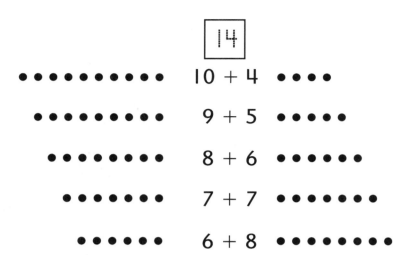

14

• • • • • • • • • •   10 + 4   • • • •

• • • • • • • • •   9 + 5   • • • • •

• • • • • • • •   8 + 6   • • • • • •

• • • • • • •   7 + 7   • • • • • • •

• • • • • •   6 + 8   • • • • • • • •

Complete for each number.

1. 13	2. 12	3. 11
10 + ☐ 3	10 + ☐	10 + ☐
9 + ☐ 4	9 + ☐	9 + ☐
8 + ☐	8 + ☐	8 + ☐
7 + ☐	7 + ☐	7 + ☐
6 + ☐	6 + ☐	6 + ☐

Complete.

4. 4 + ☐ 10 = 14

☐ 5 + 9 = 14

5. 3 + ☐ = 13

☐ + 9 = 13

6. 2 + ☐ = 12

☐ + 9 = 12

Extra Support Children may need to model the number by separating counters into two groups and recording the addition. They can then move one counter from one addend to the other and record the new fact.

Teacher Note: Use after Quick Check page 22 to reteach Unit 1, Lesson 10. **(2)**

 =  |  ≠

3	=	3		3	≠	4
1 + 2	=	3		1 + 2	≠	4

three   is equal to   three | three   is not equal to   four

Use = or ≠.

1. 6 (=) 6

5 (≠) 6

4 (=) 4

2. 10 ( ) 9

9 ( ) 9

14 ( ) 14

3. 13 ( ) 13

12 ( ) 11

8 ( ) 3

4. 2 + 2 (≠) 2

2 + 4 (=) 6

8 + 2 (=) 10

5. 6 + 3 ( ) 9

5 + 4 ( ) 11

1 + 6 ( ) 7

6. 6 + 8 ( ) 13

9 + 5 ( ) 14

4 + 10 ( ) 6

7. 3 + 4 ( ) 6

3 + 6 ( ) 9

7 + 1 ( ) 8

8. 8 + 5 ( ) 12

9 + 2 ( ) 11

7 + 5 ( ) 10

9. 5 + 5 ( ) 10

6 + 9 ( ) 14

8 + 4 ( ) 12

Extra Support Children may need to model numbers and then show a one-to-one comparison. Help children keep the numbers separate by having children model each number on its own half of a folded sheet of paper.

Teacher Note: Use after Quick Check page 30 to reteach Unit 1, Lesson 11. (2)

Comparing Numbers:
Using >, <, or =

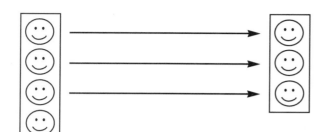 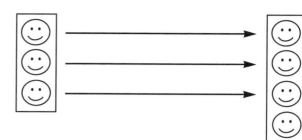

| 4 | is greater than | 3 | 3 | is less than | 4 |
| 4 | > | 3 | 3 | < | 4 |

Use > or <.

1.

5 6

2.

4 ◯ 2

3.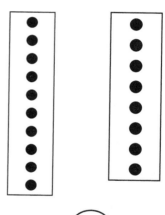

10 ◯ 8

Use >, <, or =.

4. 3 2

8 ◯ 12

6 ◯ 7

10 ◯ 10

5. 11 ◯ 7

9 ◯ 9

5 ◯ 8

9 ◯ 12

6. 9 ◯ 10

10 ◯ 2

3 ◯ 3

13 ◯ 14

Extra Support Children may have difficulty with the symbols for "is greater than" or "is less than." Point out that the side of the symbol that is "more open" points to the number that is greater.

Teacher Note: Use after Quick Check page 30 to reteach Unit 1, Lesson 12. **(2)**

Use the rule with each number in the table.

Add 4.

2	6
3	7

$2 + 4 = 6$

$3 + 4 = 7$

Subtract 2.

7	5
6	4

$7 - 2 = 5$

$6 - 2 = 4$

Complete each table.

1. Add 5.

7	12
6	11
8	13

2. Subtract 1.

14	
11	
10	

3. Subtract 4.

13	
12	
8	

4. Add 7.

7	
3	
4	

5. Subtract 4.

14	
13	
12	

6. Subtract 6.

9	
11	
10	

Extra Support Children may need to model the addition and subtraction facts using counters.

Name _____

Use tens and ones to show a number.

3 tens + 5 ones = 35   1 ten + 8 ones = 18
  30 +   5   = 35   10 +   8   = 18

Complete.

1.

   $\boxed{4}$ tens + 3 ones = $\boxed{}$

   $\boxed{40}$ +   3   = $\boxed{}$

2.

   $\boxed{}$ tens + $\boxed{}$ ones = $\boxed{}$

   $\boxed{}$ + $\boxed{}$ = $\boxed{}$

3. 6 tens + 2 ones = $\boxed{60}$ + $\boxed{2}$ = $\boxed{62}$ or sixty-two

4. 9 tens + 8 ones = $\boxed{}$ + $\boxed{}$ = $\boxed{}$ or ninety-eight

5. 2 tens + 6 ones = $\boxed{}$ + $\boxed{}$ = $\boxed{}$ or twenty-six

6. 41 = $\boxed{4}$ tens + $\boxed{1}$ one

7. 94 = $\boxed{}$ tens + $\boxed{}$ ones

8. 38 = $\boxed{}$ tens + $\boxed{}$ ones

9. 12 = $\boxed{}$ ten + $\boxed{}$ ones

10. 20 + 4 = $\boxed{24}$

11. 30 + $\boxed{}$ = 39

Extra Support Some children may need additional experience modeling tens. Have children use tens rods only to model 10, 20, 30, …100. Ask children to record the number of tens and the number each time they model. Once children are comfortable with tens, have them model numbers with tens and ones.

Teacher Note: Use after Quick Check page 50 to reteach Unit 2, Lesson 4. **(2)**

41	42	43	44	45	46	47	48	49	50
51	52	53	54	55	56	57	58	59	60

50, **51**, 52
51 is **after** 50.
51 is **before** 52.
51 is **between** 50 and 52.

Count. Complete the chart.

1.

21	22	23	24	25	26	27	28	29	30
31	32	33	34	35	36	37	38	39	40
4̶2̶	42	43			46		48	49	
	52		54	55		57			60

2. Start with 25. Skip-count by 5's. Ring those numbers.
3. Color the squares with 3 in the ones place red.
4. Color the squares with 4 in the tens place blue.

What comes before?	What comes after?	What comes between?
5. _____ , 64	6. 33, _____	7. 94, _____ , 96
_____ , 87	49, _____	39, _____ , 41
_____ , 20	20, _____	90, _____ , 92
_____ , 95	99, _____	49, _____ , 51

Extra Support Children may need to model the numbers either with blocks or by drawing the place-value blocks on a strip of paper, cutting them out, and sequencing them. Then, children can align the numbers in order, move a given number out of the row, and find the numbers before and after.

Teacher Note: Use after Quick Check page 50 to reteach Unit 2, Lesson 5. **(2)**

Reteach Worksheets

Counting by 2's

2	4	6	8	10	12	14	16	18	20

Counting by 3's

3	6	9	12	15	18	21	24	27	30

Counting by 5's

5	10	15	20	25	30	35	40	45	50

Counting by 10's

10	20	30	40	50

Complete.

1. 2, __4__, __6__, 8, __10__, __12__

2. 5, 10, ____, ____, 25, ____

3. 10, ____, ____, 40, 50, ____

4. 3, ____, ____, 12, ____, __

5. 22, 24, 26, ____, ____, ____

6. 60, 65, 70, ____, ____, ____

7. 30, 33, 36, ____, ____, ____

8. 50, 60, 70, ____, ____, ____

Extra Support Some children may see a pattern if the numbers are arranged in columns to show the pattern of the ones digits. You may wish to have children clap out a rhythmic pattern as they read each series aloud.

Teacher Note: Use after Quick Check page 50 to reteach Unit 2, Lesson 7. (2)

Rounding to the
Nearest Ten

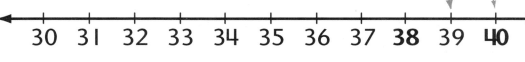

38 is closer to 40 than to 30. Round 38 to 40.

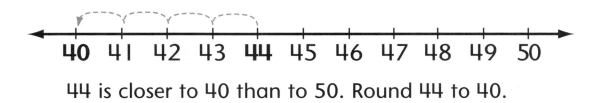

44 is closer to 40 than to 50. Round 44 to 40.

Circle the ten that is closer to the marked number.

1.
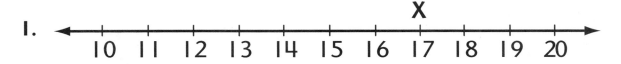

2.
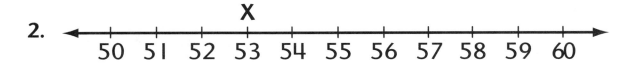

Round each number to the nearest ten.
Use the number line to help.

3.
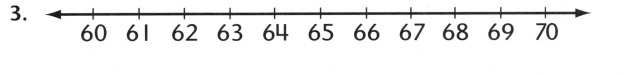

64 _____   67 _____   69 _____   62 _____   63 _____

4.
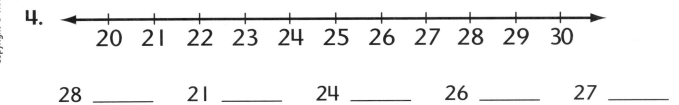

28 _____   21 _____   24 _____   26 _____   27 _____

Extra Support Children may wish to draw lines from the marked number to each ten to better visualize which ten is closer.

Teacher Note: Use after Quick Check page 58 to reteach Unit 2, Lesson 8. **(2)**

Reteach Worksheets

Name _____

Reteach 16

Counting by Dimes

 =

10¢	=	10¢
10 pennies	=	1 dime

When you count dimes, you count by 10's.

10¢   20¢   30¢   40¢   50¢

Complete.

1.

20¢ = ___20___ pennies

2.

50¢ = ___50___ pennies

3.

6 dimes = _____ ¢

4.

8 dimes = _____ ¢

5. 9 dimes = _____ ¢

6. 4 dimes = _____ ¢

7. 3 dimes = _____ ¢

8. 7 dimes = _____ ¢

Extra Support Give children 9 dimes. Remind children that when counting dimes, they count by tens. Together, have children count 9 dimes by tens. Repeat with other numbers of dimes.

84   **Teacher Note:** Use after Quick Check page 58 to reteach Unit 2, Lesson 10. **(2)**

Name _____

Problem: What do 3 dimes and 2 pennies equal? 32¢

Count dimes by tens first.   Then, count the pennies by ones.

10¢, 20¢, 30¢   31¢,   32¢

Complete.

1.

Dimes	Pennies
5	2

_____52_____ ¢

2.

Dimes	Pennies

_____ ¢

3.

Dimes	Pennies

_____ ¢

4.
Dimes	Pennies
4	6

_____ ¢

5.
Dimes	Pennies
6	8

_____ ¢

6.
Dimes	Pennies
2	7

_____ ¢

Extra Support Some children may need to review counting by tens and ones before counting dimes and pennies.

Teacher Note: Use after Quick Check page 58 to reteach Unit 2, Lesson 11. (2)

85

Problem:

$$\begin{array}{r} 5 \\ +\ 9 \\ \hline 14 \end{array} \qquad \begin{array}{r} 14 \\ -\ 9 \\ \hline \end{array}$$

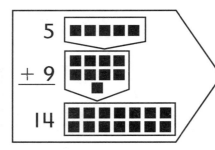

Complete.

1.
$$\begin{array}{r} 3 \\ +\ 8 \\ \hline \boxed{11} \end{array} \qquad \begin{array}{r} \boxed{11} \\ -\ 8 \\ \hline \boxed{3} \end{array}$$

2.
$$\begin{array}{r} 7 \\ +\ 8 \\ \hline \boxed{\ } \end{array} \qquad \begin{array}{r} \boxed{\ } \\ -\ 8 \\ \hline \boxed{\ } \end{array}$$

3.
$$\begin{array}{r} 9 \\ +\ 6 \\ \hline \boxed{\ } \end{array} \qquad \begin{array}{r} \boxed{\ } \\ -\ 6 \\ \hline \boxed{\ } \end{array}$$

4.
$$\begin{array}{r} 12 \\ -\ 5 \\ \hline \boxed{\ } \end{array} \qquad \begin{array}{r} \boxed{\ } \\ +\ 5 \\ \hline \boxed{\ } \end{array}$$

5.
$$\begin{array}{r} 13 \\ -\ 5 \\ \hline \boxed{\ } \end{array} \qquad \begin{array}{r} \boxed{\ } \\ +\ 5 \\ \hline \boxed{\ } \end{array}$$

6.
$$\begin{array}{r} 16 \\ -\ 8 \\ \hline \boxed{\ } \end{array} \qquad \begin{array}{r} \boxed{\ } \\ +\ 8 \\ \hline \boxed{\ } \end{array}$$

Complete. Then, write a related fact.

7. $7 + 4 = \boxed{11}$

$\underline{11 - 4 = 7}$

8. $9 + 4 = \boxed{\ }$

_____

9. $13 - 6 = \boxed{\ }$

_____

Extra Support Children may need to model each problem with counters as they write the related fact.

Teacher Note: Use after Quick Check page 76 to reteach Unit 3, Lesson 1. **(2)**

Addition Facts

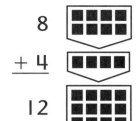

$$8$$
$$+\,4$$
$$12$$

Subtraction Facts

$$\begin{array}{r} 4 \\ +\,8 \\ \hline 12 \end{array}$$

$$\begin{array}{r} 12 \\ -\,8 \\ \hline 4 \end{array}$$

$$\begin{array}{r} 12 \\ -\,4 \\ \hline 8 \end{array}$$

Complete the fact family.

1.
$$\begin{array}{r} 6 \\ +\,8 \\ \hline 14 \end{array}$$
$$\begin{array}{r} 8 \\ +\,6 \\ \hline \boxed{14} \end{array}$$
$$\begin{array}{r} 14 \\ -\,8 \\ \hline \boxed{6} \end{array}$$
$$\begin{array}{r} 14 \\ -\,6 \\ \hline \boxed{8} \end{array}$$

2.
$$\begin{array}{r} 7 \\ +\,9 \\ \hline \boxed{} \end{array}$$
$$\begin{array}{r} 9 \\ +\,7 \\ \hline \boxed{} \end{array}$$
$$\begin{array}{r} 16 \\ -\,9 \\ \hline \boxed{} \end{array}$$
$$\begin{array}{r} 16 \\ -\,7 \\ \hline \boxed{} \end{array}$$

3.
$$\begin{array}{r} 9 \\ +\,2 \\ \hline \boxed{} \end{array}$$
$$\begin{array}{r} 2 \\ +\,9 \\ \hline \boxed{} \end{array}$$
$$\begin{array}{r} 11 \\ -\,2 \\ \hline \boxed{} \end{array}$$
$$\begin{array}{r} 11 \\ -\,9 \\ \hline \boxed{} \end{array}$$

4.
$$\begin{array}{r} 7 \\ +\,8 \\ \hline \boxed{15} \end{array}$$
$$\begin{array}{r} \boxed{8} \\ +\,\boxed{7} \\ \hline \boxed{15} \end{array}$$
$$\begin{array}{r} \boxed{15} \\ -\,\boxed{8} \\ \hline \boxed{7} \end{array}$$
$$\begin{array}{r} \boxed{15} \\ -\,\boxed{7} \\ \hline \boxed{8} \end{array}$$

5.
$$\begin{array}{r} 7 \\ +\,7 \\ \hline \boxed{} \end{array}$$
$$\begin{array}{r} \boxed{} \\ -\,\boxed{} \\ \hline \boxed{} \end{array}$$

6.
$$\begin{array}{r} 6 \\ +\,7 \\ \hline \boxed{} \end{array}$$
$$\begin{array}{r} \boxed{} \\ +\,\boxed{} \\ \hline \boxed{} \end{array}$$
$$\begin{array}{r} \boxed{} \\ -\,\boxed{} \\ \hline \boxed{} \end{array}$$
$$\begin{array}{r} \boxed{} \\ -\,\boxed{} \\ \hline \boxed{} \end{array}$$

Extra Support You may need to have children model each of the four related facts and write the fact as they complete each model.

Teacher Note: Use after Quick Check page 76 to reteach Unit 3, Lesson 2. **(2)**

Problem:
$$7 \atop {+\ 9} \atop \overline{16}$$ $$16 \atop {-\ 9}$$

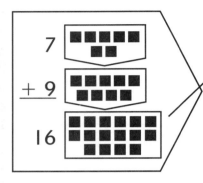
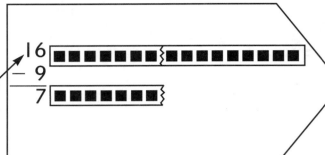
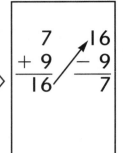

Complete.

1.
$$9 \atop {+\ 9} \atop \overline{18}$$ $$\boxed{18} \atop {-\ 9} \atop \overline{\boxed{9}}$$

2.
$$9 \atop {+\ 8} \atop \overline{\boxed{}}$$ $$\boxed{} \atop {-\ 8} \atop \overline{\boxed{}}$$

3.
$$8 \atop {+\ 8} \atop \overline{\boxed{}}$$ $$\boxed{} \atop {-\ 8} \atop \overline{\boxed{}}$$

Complete. Then write a related fact.

4. $8 + 5 = \boxed{13}$

  $13 - 5 = 8$

5. $9 + 6 = \boxed{}$

  _____

6. $14 - 5 = \boxed{}$

  _____

7.
$$4 \atop {+\ 7} \atop \overline{\boxed{11}}$$ $$\boxed{11} \atop {-\ \boxed{7}} \atop \overline{\boxed{4}}$$

8.
$$17 \atop {-\ 8} \atop \overline{\boxed{}}$$ $$\boxed{} \atop {+\ \boxed{}} \atop \overline{\boxed{}}$$

9.
$$12 \atop {-\ 9} \atop \overline{\boxed{}}$$ $$\boxed{} \atop {+\ \boxed{}} \atop \overline{\boxed{}}$$

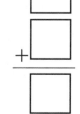

Extra Support Children may need to show the facts and related facts with counters.

Teacher Note: Use after Quick Check page 76 to reteach Unit 3, Lesson 4. **(2)**

Addition Facts

8
+ 9
17

9
+ 8
17

17

Subtraction Facts

17
− 8
9

17
− 9
8

Complete the fact family.

1.
7
+ 8
15

8
+ 7
[15]

15
− 8
[7]

15
− 7
[8]

2.
9
+ 2
☐

2
+ 9
☐

11
− 2
☐

11
− 9
☐

3.
4
+ 8
[12]

[8]
+ [4]
[12]

[12]
− [8]
[4]

[12]
− [4]
[8]

4.
9
+ 9
☐

☐
− ☐
☐

5.
7
+ 7
☐

☐
− ☐
☐

6.
6
+ 7
☐

☐
+
☐

☐
−
☐

☐
−
☐

Extra Support You may need to have children model each of the four related facts and write the fact as they complete each model.

Teacher Note: Use after Quick Check page 82 to reteach Unit 3, Lesson 5. **(2)**

Use this rule with each number in the table.

Add 6.

7	13
8	14

$7 + 6 = 13$

$8 + 6 = 14$

Subtract 8.

13	5
14	6

$13 - 8 = 5$

$14 - 8 = 6$

Complete the tables.

1. Add 7.

7	14
6	13
8	

2. Subtract 9.

16	7
17	
18	

3. Subtract 7.

14	
12	
11	

4. Add 9.

4	
6	
8	

5. Subtract 8.

17	
16	
12	

6. Subtract 5.

14	
12	
11	

Extra Support Encourage children to complete facts they know first. Children may need to model the addition and subtraction facts using counters.

Teacher Note: Use after Quick Check page 82 to reteach Unit 3, Lesson 7. **(2)**

Use tens and ones to find related facts.

 1 ten + 1 ten = ☐20

10 + 10 = **20**

2 tens − 1 ten = ☐10

20 − 10 = ☐10

1 ten + 9 ones = ☐19

10 + 9 = **19**

1 ten 9 ones − 9 ones = ☐10

19 − 9 = ☐10

1 ten + 8 ones = ☐18

10 + 8 = **18**

1 ten 8 ones − 8 ones = ☐10

18 − 8 = ☐10

Complete.

1. 1 ten + 7 ones = ☐

10 + 7 = ☐

1 ten 7 ones − 7 ones = ☐

17 − 7 = ☐

2. 10 + 6 = ☐

16 − 6 = ☐

3. 10 + 5 = ☐

15 − 5 = ☐

4. 10 + 4 = ☐

14 − 4 = ☐

5. 10 + 3 = ☐

13 − 3 = ☐

Extra Support As children model the numbers starting with 20, encourage them to verbalize the number of tens and ones and the total. Have children take away the ten each time and verbalize the pattern. Then, have them take away the ones each time and verbalize the pattern.

Teacher Note: Use after Quick Check page 84 to reteach Unit 3, Lesson 8. **(2)**

edge → corner

face

cube

8	corners
6	faces
12	edges

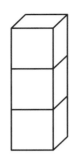 Cubes stack.

Complete.

1.

cylinder

| 0 | corners | 2 | faces | 0 | edges |

Stacks? _yes_   Rolls? _yes_

2.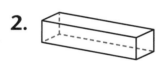

rectangular prism

| ☐ | corners | ☐ | faces | ☐ | edges |

Stacks? ____   Rolls? ____

---

3. cone

| ☐ | corners | ☐ | faces | ☐ | edges |

Stacks? ____   Rolls? ____

4.

square pyramid

| ☐ | corners | ☐ | faces | ☐ | edges |

Stacks? ____   Rolls? ____

Extra Support Children may need to handle the solids before moving to the pictorial stage. Have them touch each corner of a solid, find that corner on the picture, and point to it. Have children make a tally mark for each one they find. Repeat for faces and edges. Discuss how to record the hidden sides.

Teacher Note: Use after Quick Check page 98 to reteach Unit 4, Lesson 1. **(2)**

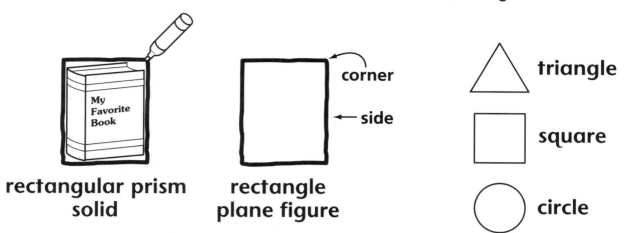

rectangular prism
solid

rectangle
plane figure

corner

side

triangle

square

circle

Trace the solid to make a plane figure.
Write the name of the face of the plane figure.

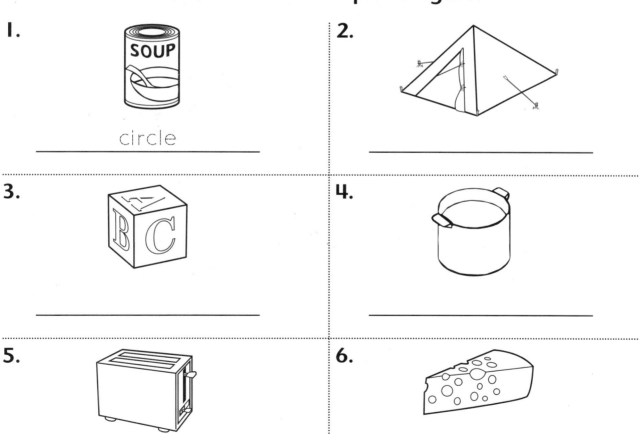

1.

circle

_____

2.

_____

3.

_____

4.

_____

5.

_____

6.

_____

Extra Support Some children may need to practice by actually tracing physical models of the solids. Encourage children to predict before they trace and to check their predictions against their results.

Teacher Note: Use after Quick Check page 98 to reteach Unit 4, Lesson 2. **(2)**

congruent   not congruent

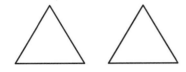   same size   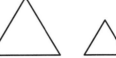   different size

same shape   same shape

symmetrical   not symmetrical

          Both parts
match.   Both parts
do not match.

Write s for same and d for different.
Write if each pair is congruent.

1.   _s_ size

   _s_ shape

Congruent? _yes_

2. 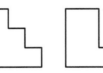   ____ size

   ____ shape

Congruent? ____

3.    ____ size

   ____ shape

Congruent? ____

4.   ____ size

   ____ shape

Congruent? ____

Ring the symmetrical figures.

5.

Extra Support Children may need to manipulate shapes to test congruence. Give children pattern blocks or other shapes, and have them show you pairs that are congruent and those that are not. To demonstrate symmetry, fold paper in half and show children how to make a heart.

Teacher Note: Use after Quick Check page 98 to reteach Unit 4, Lesson 3. **(2)**

Name _____

I shaded part $= \frac{1}{2}$
2 total parts
one half

I shaded part $= \frac{1}{3}$
3 total parts
one third

I shaded part $= \frac{1}{4}$
4 total parts
one fourth

Color one part. Complete.

1.

	1	shaded part
	2	total parts

2.

		shaded part
		total parts

3.

		shaded part
		total parts

Write the fraction for the shaded part.

part ☐　　part ☐　　part ☐

total ☐　　total ☐　　total ☐

Extra Support Some children may need to verbalize the part-whole relationship of fractions. Encourage them to describe a fraction model such as one-third as "one part out of three parts, or one third." Have children point to each fractional part and name it before asking them to write the fraction.

Teacher Note: Use after Quick Check page 108 to reteach Unit 4, Lesson 6. **(2)**

$\frac{1}{3}$ $\frac{\text{shaded part}}{\text{total parts}}$

one third

$\frac{2}{3}$ $\frac{\text{shaded parts}}{\text{total parts}}$

two thirds

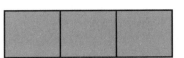

$\frac{3}{3}$ $\frac{\text{shaded parts}}{\text{total parts}}$

three thirds
the whole

Write the fraction for the shaded part.

1.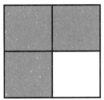

shaded parts $\dfrac{3}{4}$

total parts

2.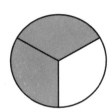

shaded parts $\dfrac{}{}$

total parts

3. 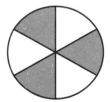 $\dfrac{}{}$

4. 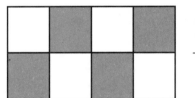 $\dfrac{}{}$

5.  $\dfrac{}{}$

6. 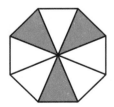 $\dfrac{}{}$

Extra Support Some children may benefit from modeling the fractions with pattern blocks or cut paper.

Teacher Note: Use after Quick Check page 108 to reteach Unit 4, Lesson 7. **(2)**

$\frac{1}{2}$ of 12 = 6 $\frac{1}{3}$ of 12 = 4 $\frac{1}{4}$ of 12 = 3

Ring $\frac{1}{2}$ of each set. Complete.

1.

$\frac{1}{2}$ of 4 = ___2___

2. ☆ ☆ ☆ ☆
☆ ☆ ☆ ☆

$\frac{1}{2}$ of 8 = _____

Ring $\frac{1}{3}$ of each set. Complete.

3. △ △ △
△ △ △

$\frac{1}{3}$ of 6 = _____

4. △ △ △ △
△ △ △ △
△ △ △ △

$\frac{1}{3}$ of 12 = _____

Ring $\frac{1}{4}$ of each set. Complete.

5. ○ ○
○ ○

$\frac{1}{4}$ of 4 = _____

6. ○ ○ ○ ○
○ ○ ○ ○

$\frac{1}{4}$ of 8 = _____

Extra Support Have children identify and model the set using counters. Then, have them separate them into equal groups. To keep the groups in order, separate them into an egg carton or other device. Have children find increasingly greater fractions of the set before working with a different fraction or a different set.

Teacher Note: Use after Quick Check page 108 to reteach Unit 4, Lesson 8. **(2)**   **97**

Reteach Worksheets

Name _____

Estimate the length.

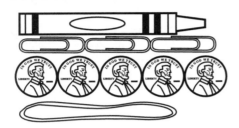

about 3 paper clips   about 4 pennies   about 1 rubber band

Now measure.

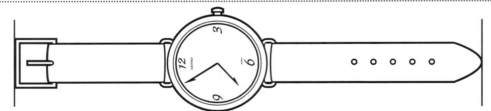

about 3 paper clips

about 5 pennies

about 1 rubber band

Estimate the lengths. Use pennies to measure.

1.

Estimate: about __8__ pennies   Measure: about __7__ pennies

2.

Estimate: about _____ pennies   Measure: about _____ pennies

Circle the tool you will use.
Measure lengths in your classroom.

3. a book

   Estimate: about _____

   Measure: about _____

4. a shoe

   Estimate: about _____

   Measure: about _____

Extra Support Some children may need a reminder to line up the end of the first paper clip, penny, or rubber band with the object being measured. It may help to have children make trains of about 10 paper clips, pennies, or rubber bands to start, measure the length, and take away or add on more objects as needed.

Teacher Note: Use after Quick Check page 122 to reteach Unit 5, Lesson 1. (2)

Each paper square is 1 inch long.
The paper train is 6 inches long.

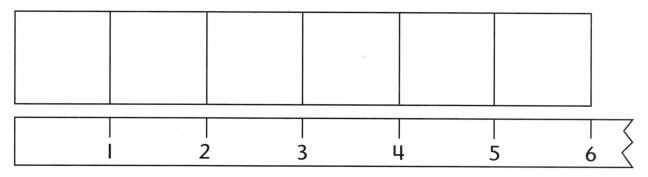

12 inches = 1 foot

Use a ruler to measure.

1.

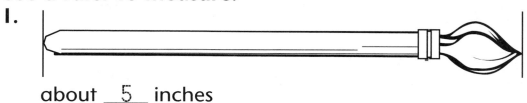

about __5__ inches

2.

about ____ inches

Use a ruler to measure in your classroom.

3.

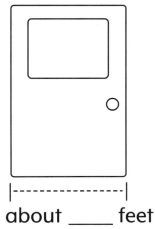

about ____ feet

4.

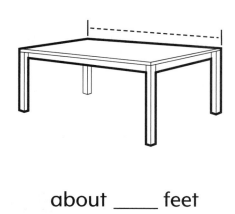

about ____ feet

Extra Support Have children model 1, 2, 3, 4 inches with 1-inch paper squares and check their measures with a ruler. Children may benefit from working in pairs to measure lengths greater than 1 foot.

Teacher Note: Use after Quick Check page 122 to reteach Unit 5, Lesson 2. **(2)**

Estimate the length. Measure the length.

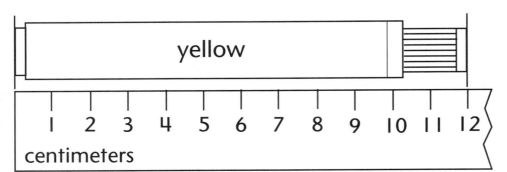

Estimate: about 10 centimeters

Measure: about 12 centimeters

A meter stick is 100 centimeters long.

100 centimeters = 1 meter

Estimate the length. Use a centimeter ruler to measure.

1.

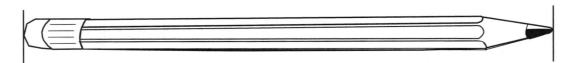

Estimate: about __15__ centimeters   Measure: about __14__ centimeters

2.

Estimate: about ____ centimeters   Measure: about ____ centimeters

Estimate and then measure the length with a meterstick.

3. length of a desk

Estimate: about ____ meters

Measure: about ____ meters

4. length of the classroom

Estimate: about _____ meters

Measure: about _____ meters

Extra Support To build knowledge of measuring with centimeters, have children make trains on their centimeter rulers using centimeter cubes. Ask them to explain how they know each length. Transition to measuring the length of objects.

Teacher Note: Use after Quick Check page 122 to reteach Unit 5, Lesson 4. **(2)**

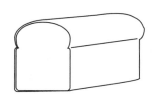

about I pound

less than I pound

more than I pound

Ring the words that tell about the object.

1.

less than   (about)   more than
I pound   I pound   I pound

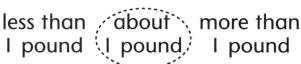

2.

less than   about   more than
I pound   I pound   I pound

3.

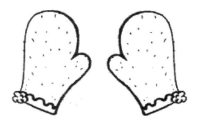

less than   about   more than
I pound   I pound   I pound

4.

less than   about   more than
I pound   I pound   I pound

Extra Support Have children hold a 1-pound object in one hand and another object in the other hand. Have them decide if the object weighs more than, about the same as, or less than 1 pound. Have children compare other objects with the 1-pound object.

Teacher Note: Use after Quick Check page 127 to reteach Unit 5, Lesson 6. (2)

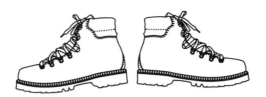

pair of boots
about 1 kilogram

less than 1 kilogram

more than 1 kilogram

Ring the words that tell about the object.

1.

less than   (about)   more than
1 kilogram   1 kilogram   1 kilogram

2.

less than   about   more than
1 kilogram   1 kilogram   1 kilogram

3.

less than   about   more than
1 kilogram   1 kilogram   1 kilogram

4.

less than   about   more than
1 kilogram   1 kilogram   1 kilogram

Extra Support Have children hold a 1-kilogram object in one hand and another object in the other hand. Have them decide if the object has a mass more than, about the same as, or less than 1 kilogram. Have children compare other objects with the 1-kilogram object.

Teacher Note: Use after Quick Check page 127 to reteach Unit 5, Lesson 7.**(2)**

 This is a cup.

 2 cups = 1 pint

2 pints = 1 quart

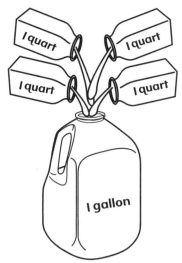 4 quarts = 1 gallon

Use a pattern to complete.

1. 2 cups = 1 pint

4 cups = 2 pints

6 cups = ⬚3⬚ pints

2. 1 quart = 2 pints

2 quarts = 4 pints

3 quarts = ⬚ pints

3. 4 pints = 8 cups

3 pints = 6 cups

⬚ pints = 4 cups

4. 4 quarts = 1 gallon

8 quarts = 2 gallons

12 quarts = ⬚ gallons

Complete.

5. ⬚ pints = 1 quart

4 pints = ⬚ quarts

6. ⬚ quarts = 1 gallon

8 quarts = ⬚ gallons

Extra Support Children may benefit from measuring with cup, pint, quart, and gallon containers.

about 1 liter

cup
less than 1 liter

watering can
more than 1 liter

Ring the words that tell about the object.

1.

less than   about   more than
1 liter   1 liter   1 liter

2.

less than   about   more than
1 liter   1 liter   1 liter

3.

less than   about   more than
1 liter   1 liter   1 liter

4.

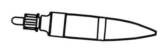

less than   about   more than
1 liter   1 liter   1 liter

5.

less than   about   more than
1 liter   1 liter   1 liter

6.

less than   about   more than
1 liter   1 liter   1 liter

Extra Support Some children may need to measure with 1-liter containers to understand the liter. Provide them with several 1-liter containers. Give children opportunities to pour from one to the other to establish their capacity before comparing containers that contain less or more.

Teacher Note: Use after Quick Check page 128 to reteach Unit 5, Lesson 9. **(2)**

A thermometer shows temperature.
There are two kinds of thermometers.
You read them the same way.

Fahrenheit   **Celsius**

Find the top of
the mercury.

Read the
number.

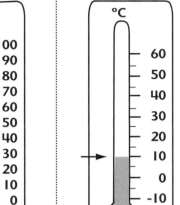

Find the top of
the mercury.

Read the
number.

40 degrees Fahrenheit   **10 degrees Celsius**

Read the thermometers.

1. Fahrenheit   **2.** Fahrenheit   **3.** Celsius

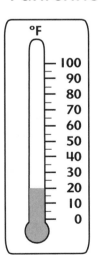   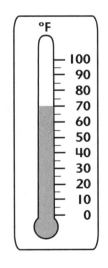   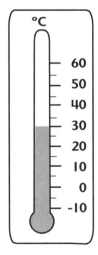

___20___ degrees   _____ degrees   _____ degrees

Extra Support Before having children read the temperature from the thermometer, have them find the numbers on the scale. Ask them to count by tens aloud as they point to each number from 0 through 100. To focus children who are easily confused visually, highlight the lines for the tens in red.

Teacher Note: Use after Quick Check page 130 to reteach Unit 5, Lesson 10. **(2)**

Name _____

Problem: 33
             + 9

Look at the tens and ones.	Add the ones. Regroup.	Add the tens.	
TENS | ONES	TENS | ONES	TENS | ONES	
3 | 3	3 | 3	3 | 3	33
+ | 9	+ | 9	+ | 9	+ 9
	| 2	4 | 2	42

Complete.

1.

T	O
3	7
+	5
4	2

2.

T	O
4	6
+	7

3.

T	O
5	7
+	5

4.

T	O
2	5
+	6

5.

T	O
6	8
+	4

6.

T	O
1	7
+	8

7.

T	O
3	4
+	8

8.

T	O
4	2
+	8

Extra Support You may have children use place-value blocks to model problem 1. First, they add the ones and regroup. Then, they add the tens to find out how many in all.

Teacher Note: Use after Quick Check page 144 to reteach Unit 6, Lesson 3. **(2)**

Name _____

Problem: 45
        +26

Look at the tens and ones.

TENS	ONES
4	5
+2	6

Add the ones. Regroup.

TENS	ONES
4	5
+ 2	6
	1

Add the tens.

TENS	ONES
4	5
+ 4	6
7	1

$$\begin{array}{r} \overset{1}{4}7 \\ +\ 26 \\ \hline 71 \end{array}$$

Complete.

1.

T	O
3	7
+ 1	3
5	0

2.

T	O
5	8
+ 2	3

3.

T	O
4	7
+ 3	5

4.

T	O
2	8
+ 1	2

5.

T	O
4	2
+ 1	8

6.

T	O
6	7
+ 2	4

7.

T	O
5	4
+ 3	8

8.

T	O
3	9
+ 3	2

Extra Support You may have children use place-value blocks to model problem 1. First, they add the ones and regroup. Then, they add the tens to find out how many in all.

Teacher Note: Use after Quick Check page 150 to reteach Unit 6, Lesson 4. **(2)**

Problem: 48
          + 5

Look at the   Add the ones.
tens and ones.   Regroup.   Add the tens.

TENS	ONES
4	8
+	5

TENS	ONES
4	8
+	5
	3

TENS	ONES
4	8
+	5
5	3

```
  ¹
  45
+ 5 8
----
  53
```

Complete.

1.
T	O
¹	
3	9
+	4
4	3

2.
T	O
5	5
+	9

3.
T	O
4	7
+	7

4.
T	O
2	8
+	6

5.
T	O
1	9
+	5

6.
T	O
6	5
+	8

7.
T	O
5	4
+	9

8.
T	O
7	8
+	6

Extra Support You may have children use place-value blocks to model problem 1. First, they add the ones and regroup. Then, they add the tens to find out how many in all.

Teacher Note: Use after Quick Check page 150 to reteach Unit 6, Lesson 5. **(2)**

Problem: 27
             + 36

Look at the tens and ones.	Add the ones. Regroup.	Add the tens.	

TENS	ONES
2	7
+ 3	6

TENS	ONES
2	7
+ 3	6
	3

TENS	ONES
2	7
+ 3	6
6	3

$$\begin{array}{r} 27 \\ + 36 \\ \hline 63 \end{array}$$

Complete.

1.

T	O
3	9
+ 1	5
5	4

2.

T	O
5	8
+ 2	6

3.

T	O
7	4
+ 1	9

4.

T	O
2	8
+ 2	5

5.

T	O
4	7
+ 3	7

6.

T	O
6	7
+ 2	6

7.

T	O
5	5
+ 3	8

8.

T	O
1	9
+ 1	4

Extra Support You may have children use place-value blocks to model problem 1. First, they add the ones and regroup. Then, they add the tens to find out how many in all.

Teacher Note: Use after Quick Check page 150 to reteach Unit 6, Lesson 6. (2)

Problem: 37
                 + 49

Look at the
tens and ones.

TENS	ONES
3	7
+ 4	9

Add the ones.
Regroup.

TENS	ONES
¹3	7
+ 4	9
	6

Add the tens.

TENS	ONES
¹3	7
+ 4	9
8	6

```
 ¹
 37
+49
―――
 86
```

Complete.

1.
T	O
3	7
+	8
4	5

2.
T	O
6	8
+	8

3.
T	O
7	6
+	6

4.
T	O
2	9
+	6

5.
T	O
4	8
+ 1	7

6.
T	O
5	7
+ 2	9

7.
T	O
4	9
+ 2	7

8.
T	O
7	8
+ 1	8

Extra Support You may have children use place-value blocks to model problem 1. First, they add the ones and regroup. Then, they add the tens to find out how many in all.

Teacher Note: Use after Quick Check page 156 to reteach Unit 6, Lesson 7. **(2)**

Problem: 47¢
         + 24¢

Look at the tens and ones.

TENS	ONES
4	7¢
+ 2	4¢

Add the ones. Regroup.

TENS	ONES
4	7¢
+ 2	4¢
	1¢

Add the tens.

TENS	ONES
4	7¢
+ 2	4¢
7	1¢

```
  47¢
+ 24¢
─────
  71¢
```

Complete.

1.   49¢
      + 19¢
      ─────
       68¢

2.   52¢
      + 38¢
      ─────

3.   15¢
      + 79¢
      ─────

4.   64¢
      + 9¢
      ─────

5.   37¢
      + 55¢
      ─────

6.   21¢
      + 49¢
      ─────

7.   33¢
      + 39¢
      ─────

8.   49¢
      + 8¢
      ─────

Extra Support   You may have children use dimes and pennies to model problem 1. First, they add the ones and regroup. Then, they add the tens. Finally, they write the cent sign.

Teacher Note: Use after Quick Check page 156 to reteach Unit 6, Lesson 9.   **(2)**

Problem: 32
            45
          + 19

Look at the
tens and ones.

TENS	ONES
3	2
4	5
+ 1	9

Add the ones.
Regroup.

TENS	ONES
3	2
4	5
+ 1	9
	6

Add the tens.

TENS	ONES
3	2
4	5
+ 1	9
9	6

```
  1
  32
  45
+ 19
  96
```

Complete.

1.   1
      25
      33
    + 18
      76

2.   39
      16
    + 10

3.   48
      22
    + 13

4.   56
      17
    + 14

5.   19
      38
    + 22

6.   20
      55
    + 19

7.   47
      28
    + 23

8.   54
      10
    + 18

Extra Support You may have children use place-value blocks to model problem 1. Remind them to add from top to bottom. First, they add the ones and regroup. Then, they add the tens to find out how many in all.

Teacher Note: Use after page 158 to reteach Unit 6, Lesson 10. **(2)**

Name _____

Problem: 3 1
           − 6

Look at the   Regroup a ten.
tens and ones.   Subtract the ones.   Subtract the tens.

TENS	ONES
3	1
−	6

TENS	ONES
$\frac{2}{3}$	$\frac{11}{1}$
−	6
	5

TENS	ONES
$\frac{2}{3}$	$\frac{11}{1}$
−	6
2	5

$$\begin{array}{r}\overset{2}{\cancel{3}}\,\overset{11}{\cancel{1}}\\ -\quad 6\\ \hline 2\,5\end{array}$$

Complete.

1.

T	O
$\overset{4}{\cancel{5}}$	$\overset{11}{\cancel{1}}$
−	8
4	3

2.

T	O
7	2
−	6

3.

T	O
3	1
−	9

4.

T	O
2	2
−	4

5.

T	O
4	1
−	5

6.

T	O
5	2
−	7

7.

T	O
6	1
−	7

8.

T	O
8	2
−	9

Extra Support You may have children use place-value blocks to model problem 1. First, they regroup a ten. Then, they subtract the ones. Finally, they subtract the tens to find out how many are left.

Teacher Note: Use after Quick Check page 172 to reteach Unit 7, Lesson 3. **(2)**   **113**

Name_____

Problem: 32
            − 19

Look at the tens and ones.	Regroup a ten. Subtract the ones.	Subtract the tens.	

TENS	ONES
3	2
− 1	9

TENS	ONES
2̷3	12 2̷
− 1	9
	3

TENS	ONES
2̷3	12 2̷
− 1	9
1	3

```
   2 12
   3̷ 2̷
 − 1 9
   1 3
```

Complete.

1.

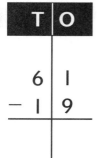

T	O
6	11
7̷	2̷
− 3	8
3	3

2.

T	O
9	1
− 2	5

3.

T	O
5	2
− 2	7

4.

T	O
7	2
− 3	8

5.

T	O
6	1
− 1	9

6.

T	O
9	2
− 6	6

7.

T	O
4	1
− 1	7

8.

T	O
7	2
− 5	4

Extra Support You may have children use place-value blocks to model problem 1. First, they regroup a ten. Then, they subtract the ones. Finally, they subtract the tens to find out how many are left.

2-Digit Subtraction:
Regrouping 10

Problem: 40
          − 26

Look at the   Regroup a ten.
tens and ones.   Subtract the ones. Subtract the tens.

TENS	ONES
4	0
− 2	6

TENS	ONES
³4̶	¹⁰0̶
− 2	6
	4

TENS	ONES
³4̶	¹⁰0̶
− 2	6
1	4

```
  3 10
  4̶ 0̶
− 2 6
  1 4
```

Complete.

1.

T	O
6	10
7̶	0̶
− 3	5
3	5

2.

T	O
9	0
− 2	8

3.

T	O
8	1
− 2	7

4.

T	O
5	0
− 1	4

5.

T	O
6	2
− 1	9

6.

T	O
4	0
− 2	9

7.

T	O
8	0
− 4	3

8.

T	O
3	0
− 2	2

Extra Support You may have children use place-value blocks to model problem 1. First, they regroup a ten. Then, they subtract the ones. Finally, they subtract the tens to find out how many are left.

Teacher Note: Use after Quick Check page 178 to reteach Unit 7, Lesson 5. (2)

Problem: 70¢
          − 48¢

Look at the   Regroup a ten.
tens and ones.   Subtract the ones. Subtract the tens.

TENS	ONES
7	0¢
− 4	8¢

TENS	ONES
⁶7̷	¹⁰0̷¢
− 4	8¢
	2¢

TENS	ONES
⁶7̷	¹⁰0̷¢
− 4	8¢
2	2¢

```
  6 10
  7 0̷¢
 −4 8¢
 ─────
  2 2¢
```

Solve.

1. Had: 72¢

   Bought:

   Had __33__ ¢ left

2. Had: 80¢

   Bought:

   Had _____ ¢ left

3. Had: 91¢

   Bought:

   Had _____ ¢ left

4. Had: 52¢

   Bought:

   Had _____ ¢ left

5. Had: 60¢

   Bought:

   Had _____ ¢ left

6. Had: 81¢

   Bought:

   Had _____ ¢ left

Extra Support You may have children use dimes and pennies to model problem 1. First, they regroup and subtract the ones. Then, they subtract the tens and find out how much is left. Finally, they write the cent sign.

Problem: 53
              − 8

Look at the
tens and ones.

Regroup a ten.
Subtract the ones.

Subtract the tens.

TENS	ONES
5	3
−	8

TENS	ONES
⁴5̷	¹³3̷
−	8
	5

TENS	ONES
⁴5̷	¹³3̷
−	8
4	5

⁴5̷ ¹³3̷
−   8
4 5

Complete.

1.

T	O
7	14
8	4̷
−	8
7	6

2.

T	O
7	3
−	6

3.

T	O
3	3
−	9

4.

T	O
2	4
−	5

5.

T	O
4	3
−	5

6.

T	O
5	4
−	7

7.

T	O
6	3
−	7

8.

T	O
8	3
−	8

Extra Support You may have children use place-value blocks to model problem 1. First, they regroup a ten.
Then, they subtract the ones. Finally, they subtract the tens to find out how many are left.

Reteach 50

2-Digit Subtraction:
Regrouping 13 and 14

Problem: 44
             − 25

Look at the   Regroup a ten.
tens and ones.   Subtract the ones. Subtract the tens.

TENS	ONES
4	4
− 2	5

TENS	ONES
³4̷	¹⁴4̷
− 2	5
	9

TENS	ONES
³4̷	¹⁴4̷
− 2	5
1	9

$$\begin{array}{r} \overset{3}{\cancel{4}}\,\overset{14}{\cancel{4}} \\ -2\,5 \\ \hline 1\,9 \end{array}$$

Complete.

1.
T	O
⁶	¹³
7̸	3̸
− 3	5
3	8

2.
T	O
9	4
− 2	7

3.
T	O
8	4
− 3	7

4.
T	O
7	3
− 1	8

5.
T	O
6	3
− 1	9

6.
T	O
4	4
− 1	5

7.
T	O
5	4
− 2	9

8.
T	O
3	3
− 1	6

Extra Support   You may have children use place-value blocks to model problem 1. First, they regroup a ten. Then, they subtract the ones. Finally, they subtract the tens to find out how many are left.

Teacher Note: Use after Quick Check page 186 to reteach Unit 7, Lesson 8 **(2)**

Problem: 65
         −39

Look at the
tens and ones.

Regroup a ten.
Subtract the ones.

Subtract the tens.

TENS	ONES
6	5
−3	9

TENS	ONES
⁵6̸	¹⁵5̸
−3	9
	6

TENS	ONES
⁵6̸	¹⁵5̸
−3	9
2	6

```
  5 15
  6̸ 5̸
− 3 9
─────
  2 6
```

Complete.

1.

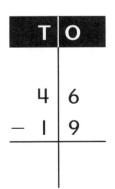

	T	O
	⁶7̸	¹⁶6̸
−	3	7
	3	9

2.

	T	O
	9	5
−	5	7

3.

	T	O
	6	6
−	3	8

4.

	T	O
	5	5
−	1	8

5.

	T	O
	4	6
−	1	9

6.

	T	O
	8	6
−	4	9

7.

	T	O
	3	6
−	1	7

8.

	T	O
	8	5
−	6	6

Extra Support You may have children use place-value blocks to model problem 1. First, they regroup a ten. Then, they subtract the ones. Finally, they subtract the tens to find out how many are left.

Teacher Note: Use after Quick Check page 186 to reteach Unit 7, Lesson 10. **(2)**

Problem: 65
            −38

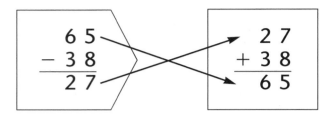

Subtract. Check by adding.

1.

$$\begin{array}{r} 53 \\ -29 \\ \hline 24 \end{array} \qquad \begin{array}{r} 24 \\ +29 \\ \hline 53 \end{array}$$

2.

$$\begin{array}{r} 48 \\ -19 \\ \hline \end{array} \qquad \begin{array}{r} \\ + \\ \hline \end{array}$$

3.

$$\begin{array}{r} 77 \\ -29 \\ \hline \end{array} \qquad \begin{array}{r} \\ + \\ \hline \end{array}$$

4.

$$\begin{array}{r} 50 \\ -31 \\ \hline \end{array} \qquad \begin{array}{r} \\ + \\ \hline \end{array}$$

5.

$$\begin{array}{r} 62 \\ -45 \\ \hline \end{array} \qquad \begin{array}{r} \\ + \\ \hline \end{array}$$

6.

$$\begin{array}{r} 84 \\ -67 \\ \hline \end{array} \qquad \begin{array}{r} \\ + \\ \hline \end{array}$$

Extra Support You may need to tell children that the difference in the subtraction problem becomes the first addend in the addition problem.

Teacher Note: Use after Quick Check page 192 to reteach Unit 7, Lesson 12. **(2)**

Problem: 34 + 18 = _____

| 34 + 18 | 34 $+18$ | 34 $+18$ $\overline{52}$ |

Write the problem vertically. Solve.

1. 42 + 29 = _____

$$\begin{array}{r} 42 \\ +29 \\ \hline 71 \end{array}$$

2. 61 − 15 = _____

3. 56 + 28 = _____

4. 38 + 47 = _____

5. 70 − 43 = _____

6. 83 − 19 = _____

7. 40 − 16 = _____

8. 58 + 39 = _____

9. 22 + 28 = _____

Extra Support Remind children to line up the tens and ones when they write problems vertically.

Teacher Note: Use after Quick Check page 192 to reteach Unit 7, Lesson 13. **(2)**

The hour hand shows
what hour it is.

hour hand

3 o'clock

Ring the correct time.

1.

(8:00)   12:00

2.

11:00   10:00

3.

6:00   12:00

4.

12 o'clock   2 o'clock

5.

5 o'clock   10 o'clock

6.

1 o'clock   11 o'clock

Extra Support Tell children that the hour hand is the shorter hand and that the number it points to tells the hour.

Teacher Note: Use after Quick Check page 204 to reteach Unit 8, Lesson 1. **(2)**

A half-hour is 30 minutes.
2:30 means **30** minutes
after 2 o'clock, or half past 2.

2:00

2:30

Ring the correct time.

1.

(4:30)   5:30

2.

12:30   1:30

3.

9:30   10:30

4.

half past 3

half past 4

5.

half past 6

half past 7

6.

half past 1

half past 2

Extra Support Remind children that when showing a time to the half hour, the minute hand points to the 6 and the hour hand is between two numbers.

Teacher Note: Use after Quick Check page 204 to reteach Unit 8, Lesson 2. **(2)**

It is **15** minutes **after** 7.
It is **quarter past** 7.

7:00

7:15

Ring the correct time.

1.

(6:15)   7:15

2.

1:15   2:15

3.

8:15   9:15

4.

quarter past 4

quarter past 5

5.

quarter past 9

quarter past 10

6.

quarter past 11

quarter past 12

Extra Support Review counting by 5's on the clock until 15 minutes past. Remind children that the minute hand points to the 3 and the hour hand is just past a number when showing quarter past an hour.

Teacher Note: Use after Quick Check page 204 to reteach Unit 8, Lesson 3. **(2)**

Name _____

It is **45** minutes **after 5**.
It is **quarter to 6**.

5:00

5:45

6:00

Ring the correct time.

1.

1:45   (2:45)

2.

10:45   11:45

3.

6:45   7:45

4.

quarter to 6

quarter to 7

5.

quarter to 9

quarter to 10

6.

quarter to 3

quarter to 4

Extra Support Review counting by 5's on the clock until 45 minutes after. Tell children that 45 minutes *after* an hour is the same as quarter to, or 15 minutes *before*, the next hour.

Teacher Note: Use after Quick Check page 210 to reteach Unit 8, Lesson 4. **(2)**

Name_____

There are 60 minutes in a hour.

9:00

It is 5 minutes past 9.

9:05

It is 25 minutes past 9.

9:25

Complete.

1.

__10__ minutes past 3

2.

_____ minutes past 11

3.

_____ minutes past 7

4.

_____ minutes past 8

5.

_____ minutes past 2

6.

_____minutes past 10

Extra Support You may need to tell children to point to each number on the clock, starting with the 1, and count by 5's to find the minutes after the hour.

Teacher Note: Use after Quick Check page 210 to reteach Unit 8, Lesson 5. **(2)**

1 hour later   **2 hours later**   **3 hours later**

5:00   6:00   7:00   8:00

Complete.

1.

   to

__3__ hours later

2.

   to

_____ hours later

3.

   to

_____ hour later

Extra Support Remind children to look at the hour hand and count on from the starting hour to find how many hours later.

Teacher Note: Use after Quick Check page 210 to reteach Unit 8, Lesson 6. (2)

The **month** is May.

The **sixteenth day** is a **Tuesday.**

May

Sunday	Monday	Tuesday	Wednesday	Thursday	Friday	Saturday
	1	2	3	4	5	6
7	8	9	10	11	12	13
14	15	16	17	18	19	20
21	22	23	24	25	26	27
28	29	30	31			

Use the calendar. Ring the correct answer.

1. What is the name of this month?   June   (May)   April

2. How many days are in this month?   7   31   16

3. How many days are in a week?   31   7   100

4. When is the eighteenth day in this month?   Monday   Tuesday   Thursday

Extra Support You may need to remind children of the ordinal number words *first* through *twentieth* and the corresponding numbers 1 through 20. You may also need to remind children to look at the top of a column to find the day of the week for any date in that column.

Teacher Note: Use after Quick Check page 218 to reteach Unit 8, Lesson 8. **(2)**

nickel

5¢

Count on
by **5's.**

5¢   10¢

dime

10¢

Count on
by **10's.**

10¢   20¢

Count the money. Ring how much in all.

1.

___5___ ¢ , ___10___ ¢ , ___15___ ¢   (15¢)   5¢

2.

_____ ¢ , _____ ¢ , _____ ¢   10¢   30¢

3.

_____ ¢ , _____ ¢   10¢   15¢

Extra Support Children may need to write the value of each coin before they find the total. Remind them to count on by 5's for each nickel and by 10's for each dime.

Teacher Note: Use after Quick Check page 218 to reteach Unit 8, Lesson 9. **(2)**

Name_____

dime	nickel	penny
10¢	5¢	1¢

10¢,   20¢,   25¢,   26¢,   27¢,   28¢ | 28¢ in all |

Count the money. Ring how much in all.

1.

___10___ ¢ , ___20___ ¢ , ___25___ ¢ , ___26___ ¢   (26¢)   30¢

2.

_____ ¢ , _____ ¢ , _____ ¢ , _____ ¢   40¢   21¢

3.

_____ ¢ , _____ ¢ , _____ ¢ , _____ ¢   17¢   13¢

Extra Support Remind children to count on by 10's for each dime, 5's for each nickel, and 1's for each penny.

Teacher Note: Use after Quick Check page 218 to reteach Unit 8, Lesson 10. **(2)**

Name _____

quarter	dime	nickel	penny

25¢	10¢	5¢	1¢

Start with 25.
Count on.

25¢   26¢

total
26¢

Count. Ring the total.

1.

‎ 25 ‎ ‎ ‎ ‎ 30
_____ ¢ , _____ ¢   26¢   (30¢)

2.

_____ ¢ , _____ ¢   35¢   25¢

3.

_____ ¢ , _____ ¢ , _____ ¢   45¢   36¢

Extra Support Children may need more time using coins when finding the total. You may need to remind children that the value of a quarter is 25¢, and to count on by 10's for each dime, 5's for each nickel, and 1's for each penny.

Teacher Note: Use after Quick Check page 222 to reteach Unit 8, Lesson 11. **(2)**   **131**

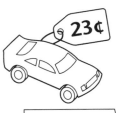 

The total cost is 36¢.
There is enough money.

Find the total cost. Do you have enough money?
Ring yes or no.

1.

12¢
+15¢

yes   no

2.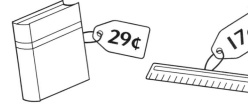

29¢
+17¢

yes   no

3.

16¢
+28¢

yes   no

4.

21¢
+11¢

yes   no

Extra Support You may need to remind children how to add money by adding the ones, regrouping if necessary, and then adding the tens. Children may need more experience finding the total cost and comparing that cost to the total amount of money available.

Teacher Note: Use after Quick Check page 222 to reteach Unit 8, Lesson 12. **(2)**

You buy: You have:

13¢   10¢

Add.   Subtract.

13¢   25¢ amount you have
+10¢   −23¢ total cost
23¢   total cost   2¢ in change

How much change do you get back?

1. You buy: 17¢   You have:
    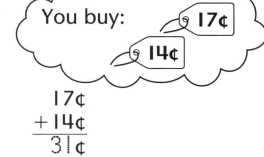 14¢

    17¢   35¢
    +14¢   −31¢
    31¢   _____ ¢ in change

2. You buy: 14¢   You have:
    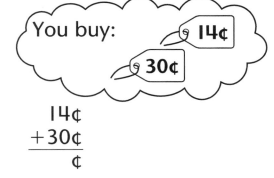 30¢

    14¢   45¢
    +30¢   −___ ¢
    _____ ¢   _____ ¢ in change

Extra Support You may need to remind children how to solve a two-step problem. First, they add to find the total cost of the items they buy. Then, they subtract the total cost from the amount of money they have to find how much change.

Teacher Note: Use after Quick Check page 222 to reteach Unit 8, Lesson 13. **(2)**

Name_____

There are 3 pennies in the bank.

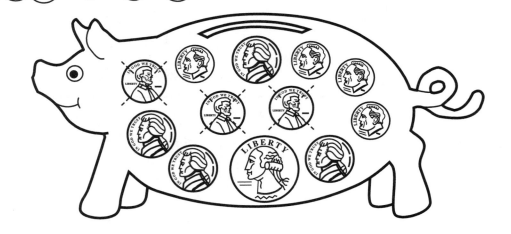

Look at the picture. Cross out each coin when you make a tally mark.

1.	penny	|||	3
2.	nickel		
3.	dime		
4.	quarter		

Extra Support Remind children to cross out one penny, make a tally mark for it, cross out another penny, make a tally mark for it, and so on, until all of the pennies have been crossed out and tallied. Have them repeat the process for nickels, dimes, and quarters.

Teacher Note: Use after Quick Check page 236 to reteach Unit 9, Lesson 1. **(2)**

Here is a survey of **9** people.
Each person chose one favorite activity.

Sue and Fred chose skating.
Bob, Carol, and Jack chose swimming.
Tam, Sam, Tom, and Lu chose biking.

Two people chose skating.

| |

Complete the chart. Then ring the correct answer.

1. skating			
skating		I I	2
2. swimming			
3. biking			

4. Which activity was chosen the most?   swimming   biking

5. Which activity was chosen the least?   biking   skating

Extra Support You may need to tell children to make one tally mark for each person in the survey. First, they make a tally mark for each person who chose skating. Then, they make a tally mark for each person who chose swimming. Finally, they make a tally mark for each person who chose biking.

Teacher Note: Use after Quick Check page 236 to reteach Unit 9, Lesson 2. (2)

Number of Children in Each Scout Troop	
Troop 2B	卌　　卌	
Troop 2J	卌　　|||
Troop 2S	卌　　卌　　卌

Number of Children in Each Scout Troop

	0	1	2	3	4	5	6	7	8	9	10	11	12	13	14	15
Troop 2B																
Troop 2J																
Troop 2S																

There are 11 children in Troop 2B.

Use the tally chart to complete the graph. Solve.

Number of Children in Each Club	
Book Club	卌	
Bike Club	卌　　卌
Computer Club	卌

1.　　### Number of Children in Each Club

	0	1	2	3	4	5	6	7	8	9	10
Book Club											
Bike Club											
Computer Club											

2. How many children are in the Book Club?　　(6)　　8

3. How many children are in the Computer Club?　　5　　10

Extra Support You may need to tell children to color in one box for each tally mark. They can check that they have organized the data correctly by checking that the numbers of boxes colored in are the same as the numbers on the tally chart.

　　Teacher Note: Use after Quick Check page 236 to reteach Unit 9, Lesson 3. (2)

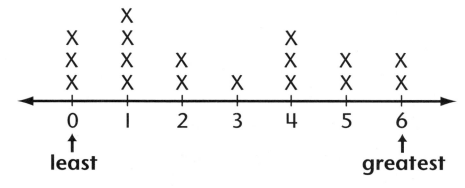

Number of Days Absent for Children in Class 2K

Each X stands for 1 child.

> I day has the greatest number of X's.
> I is the **mode**.

> The greatest number of days is 6.
> The least number of days is 0.
> 6 – 0 = 6. The **range** is 6.

Use the line plot. Ring the correct word to complete.

1. I day has the _____ number of X's.   least   (greatest)

2. I is the _____ .   range   mode

3. The _____ number of days is 6.   least   greatest

4. The _____ number of days is 0.   least   greatest

5. Six minus zero equals _____.   six   zero

6. The _____ is 6.   range   mode

Extra Support You may need to tell children that they can find the mode by first finding the column with the greatest number of X's in it and then finding the number below that column. They can find the range by subtracting the least number on the line plot from the greatest number.

Teacher Note: Use after Quick Check page 238 to reteach Unit 9, Lesson 4. (2)   **137**

Always	Sometimes	Never
		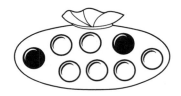

You will **always** pick a white marble.   You will **sometimes** pick a black marble.   You will **never** pick a gray marble.

Solve.

1. You will pick a black marble from the bag.

always   sometimes   never

2. You will pick a gray marble from the bag.

always   sometimes   never

3. You will pick a white marble from the bag.

always   sometimes   never

4. You will pick a white marble from the bag.

always   sometimes   never

Extra Support Discuss with children strategies to determine the likeliness of an event. Have them use marbles to test out their predictions.

Teacher Note: Use after Quick Check page 242 to reteach Unit 9, Lesson 6. **(2)**

How many hundreds? How many tens? How many ones?

___1___ hundred   ___0___ tens   ___6___ ones

Complete the table.

	Hundreds	Tens	Ones	Number
1.	1	0	1	101
2.	1	0	2	
3.	1	0	3	
4.	1	0	4	
5.	1	0	5	
6.	1	0	6	
7.	1	0	7	
8.	1	0	8	
9.	1	0	9	

Extra Support You may want to remind children that in a number such as 102, they must write 0 as a place holder between the hundreds and the ones places because there are no tens. Explain that even though they say "one hundred two," they must write a zero to show that there are no tens.

Teacher Note: Use after Quick Check page 254 to reteach Unit 10, Lesson 2. **(2)**

As you go across each row, each number is greater by 1.

As you go down each column, each number is greater by 10.

101	102	103	104	105	106	107	108	109	110
111	112	113	114	115	116	117	118	119	120
121	122	123	124	125	126	127	128	129	130
131	132	133	134	135	136	137	138	139	140
141	142	143	144	145	146	147	148	149	150
151	152	153	154	155	156	157	158	159	160

Write the missing numbers.

1. _111_ , ____ , 113 , ____ , ____ , ____ , ____ , ____ , 119 , ____

2. 137 , ____ , ____ , ____ , ____ , ____ , 143 , ____ , ____ , ____

3. ____ , ____ , ____ , 161 , ____ , ____ , ____ , ____ , ____ , 167

4. ____ , 170 , ____ , ____ , ____ , ____ , ____ , 176 , ____ , ____

5. ____ , ____ , ____ , 121 , ____ , ____ , ____ , 125 , ____ , ____

6. ____ , 128 , ____ , ____ , ____ , ____ , 133 , ____ , ____ , ____

7. ____ , ____ , 193 , ____ , ____ , ____ , ____ , ____ , 199 , ____

8. 179 , ____ , ____ , ____ , ____ , 184 , ____ , ____ , ____ , ____

Extra Support Some children may need to count aloud to find the missing numbers. Others may need to use the number chart to help them. They can place a counter on each number as they count.

Teacher Note: Use after Quick Check page 254 to reteach Unit 10, Lesson 3. (2)

You can show a number with blocks.
You can write a number 3 ways.

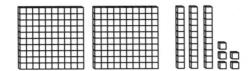

___2___ hundreds ___3___ tens ___5___ ones

___200___ + ___30___ + ___5___ = ___235___

Complete.

1.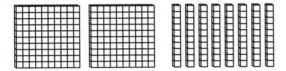

___2___ hundreds ___8___ tens ___0___ ones

___200___ + ___80___ + ___0___ = ___280___

2.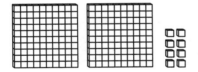

_____ hundreds _____ tens _____ ones

_____ + _____ + _____ = _____

3.   243

_____ hundreds _____ tens _____ ones

_____ + _____ + _____ = _____

Extra Support Some children may need to use place-value blocks to model the numbers.

Teacher Note: Use after Quick Check page 260 to reteach Unit 10, Lesson 4. **(2)**

141

Reteach Worksheets

You can show a number with blocks.
You can write a number 3 ways.

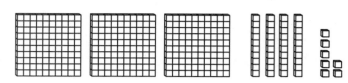

___3___ hundreds ___4___ tens ___7___ ones

___300___ + ___40___ + ___7___ = ___347___

Complete.

1.

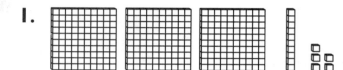

___3___ hundreds ___1___ ten ___5___ ones

___300___ + ___10___ + ___5___ = ___315___

2.

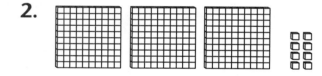

_____ hundreds _____ tens _____ ones

_____ + _____ + _____ = _____

3. **353**

_____ hundreds _____ tens _____ ones

_____ + _____ + _____ = _____

Extra Support Some children may need to use place-value blocks to model the numbers.

Teacher Note: Use after Quick Check page 260 to reteach Unit 10, Lesson 5. **(2)**

● You can show a number with blocks.
You can write a number 3 ways.

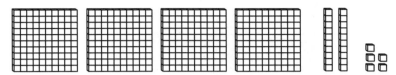

___4___ hundreds ___2___ tens ___5___ ones

___400___ + ___20___ + ___5___ = ___425___

Complete.

1.

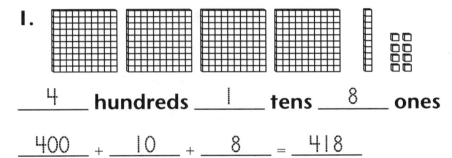

___4___ hundreds ___1___ tens ___8___ ones

___400___ + ___10___ + ___8___ = ___418___

2.

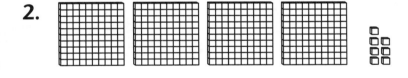

_____ hundreds _____ tens _____ ones

_____ + _____ + _____ = _____

3.   473

_____ hundreds _____ tens _____ ones

_____ + _____ + _____ = _____

Extra Support Some children may need to use place-value blocks to model the numbers.

Teacher Note: Use after Quick Check page 260 to reteach Unit 10, Lesson 6. **(2)**

You can write 5 I cents
in two ways.

You can use a **cent sign**.

You can use a **dollar sign**
and a **decimal point**.

51¢ $.51

Write the amount in two ways.

1.

_28_ ¢

$ _.28_

2.

_____ ¢

$ ___.___

3.

_____ ¢

$ ___.___

4.

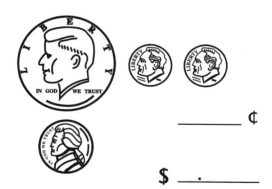

_____ ¢

$ ___.___

Extra Support Some children may have difficulty keeping track of the coins they have counted. You may want to suggest that they mark an X on each coin as they count.

Teacher Note: Use after Quick Check page 269 to reteach Unit 10, Lesson 9. **(2)**

Count by 10's to find the value of the dimes.

10 dimes = 100¢ = 1 dollar or $1.00

Write the amount.

1.   **2.**

$ _2.00_ $ ___.___

3.   **4.**

$ ___.___

$ ___.___

Write the amount.

5. 1 dollar and 2 dimes = $ ___.___

6. 7 dollars and 5 dimes = $ ___.___

Extra Support You may need to explain that the dollars are counted and written separately from the coins.

Teacher Note: Use after Quick Check page 269 to reteach Unit 10, Lesson 10. **(2)**

2 dollars   I dime   4 pennies

$ _2.14_

Complete.

1.

   dollars dimes pennies

_1_   _0_   _3_ = $ _1.03_

....

2. 8 dollars I dime 0 pennies is $ _____._____

3. 4 dollars 0 dimes 9 pennies is $ _____._____

4. I dollar 6 dimes 9 pennies is $ _____._____

5. 5 dollars 8 dimes 7 pennies is $ _____._____

6. 9 dollars I dime 0 pennies is $ _____._____

Extra Support You may need to remind children that dollars are counted first, then the coins.

1 half-dollar = $.50   2 quarters = 1 half-dollar = $.50

2 half-dollars = $1.00   4 quarters = $1.00

Ring the correct amount.

1.

$1.00   ($.50) $.25

2.

$.50 $1.00 $.25

3.

$.75 $1.50 $1.00

4.

$.50 $1.00 $1.25

Extra Support You may want children to make their own equivalent-value charts for $1.00.

Name _____

Adding and Subtracting
1-Digit Numbers

Problem: 1 3 2
            +   7
            _____

Problem: 2 4 8
            −   5
            _____

Add the ones.
Add the tens.
Add the hundreds.

H	T	O
1	3	2
+		7
1	3	9

```
  1 3 2
+     7
_____
  1 3 9
```

Subtract the ones.
Subtract the tens.
Subtract the hundreds.

H	T	O
2	4	8
−		5
2	4	3

```
  2 4 8
−     5
_____
  2 4 3
```

Add or subtract.

1.

H	T	O
2	3	5
+		4

2.

H	T	O
1	3	9
−		7

3.

H	T	O
2	3	7
−		2

4.

H	T	O
7	3	6
+		2

5.   2 4 2
        +   6
        _____

6.   3 6 4
        −   3
        _____

7.   9 7 1
        −   1
        _____

8.   8 2 7
        +   2
        _____

9.   1 9 8
        −   7
        _____

10.   5 6 6
         −   3
         _____

11.   7 8 3
         +   6
         _____

12.   2 9 6
         −   4
         _____

13.   6 3 4
         +   4
         _____

14.   1 7 2
         +   7
         _____

Extra Support You may want to have children review addition and subtraction facts before beginning this page.

Teacher Note: Use after Quick Check page 282 to reteach Unit 11, Lesson 1. **(2)**

Name _____

Reteach 81

Adding and Subtracting
2-Digit Numbers

Reteach Worksheets

Problem: 2 1 4
         +   1 2

Add the ones.
Add the tens.
Add the hundreds.

H	T	O
2	1	4
+	1	2
2	2	6

    2 1 4
  +   1 2
    2 2 6

Problem: 1 5 6
         −   2 4

Subtract the ones.
Subtract the tens.
Subtract the hundreds.

H	T	O
1	5	6
−	2	4
1	3	2

    1 5 6
  −   2 4
    1 3 2

Add or subtract.

1.
H	T	O
2	9	4
−	8	1
2	1	3

2.
H	T	O
6	2	9
+	7	0

3.
H	T	O
4	5	8
−	5	3

4.
H	T	O
3	4	1
+	3	5

5.
H	T	O
8	5	5
+	3	3

6.
H	T	O
1	3	9
−	2	7

7.
H	T	O
5	3	2
+	6	1

8.
H	T	O
1	7	6
−	7	6

9.   9 0 3
       +   9 5

10.   7 5 2
        −   3 0

11.   8 4 0
        +   2 7

12.   4 6 5
        −   6 4

13.   5 7 8
        −   5 3

Extra Support Some children may need to draw lines between the hundreds, tens, and ones columns in order to write the sums and differences in the proper place. You may have children circle the plus or minus signs to make sure they perform the correct operation.

Teacher Note: Use after Quick Check page 282 to reteach Unit 11, Lesson 2. **(2)**

Copyright © Houghton Mifflin Company. All rights reserved.

Name_____

3-Digit Addition with
Regrouping

Problem: 1 3 7
           + 2 2 6

Look at the
hundreds, tens,
and ones.

Add the ones.
Regroup.
Add the tens.

Add the hundreds.

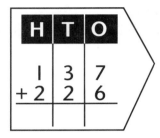

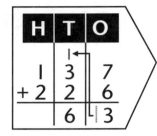

H	T	O
	1	
	3	7
+ 2	2	6
3	6	3

```
    1
  137
+ 226
  363
```

Add.

1.

H	T	O
	1	
6	4	5
+ 2	3	5
8	8	0

2.

H	T	O
3	8	2
+ 4	0	8

3.

H	T	O
2	3	9
+ 1	4	7

4.

H	T	O
1	4	8
+ 3	3	9

5.

H	T	O
4	5	8
+ 3	2	3

6.

H	T	O
4	3	9
+ 1	4	6

7.

H	T	O
1	2	7
+ 5	5	3

8.

H	T	O
5	6	4
+ 3	2	7

Extra Support Remind children to write the regrouped ten at the top of the tens column so they won't forget to add it when they add the tens.

Teacher Note: Use after Quick Check page 288 to reteach Unit 11, Lesson 4. **(2)**

Problem: 254
-128

Look at the hundreds, tens, and ones.

Regroup a ten.
Subtract the ones.
Subtract the tens. Subtract the hundreds.

H	T	O
2	5	4
– 1	2	8

H	T	O
	4	14
2	5̸	4
– 1	2	8
	2	6

H	T	O
	4	14
2	5̸	4
– 1	2	8
1	2	6

$$\begin{array}{r} 4\,14 \\ 2\,5\!\!\!/\,4 \\ -1\,2\,8 \\ \hline 1\,2\,6 \end{array}$$

Complete.

1.

H	T	O
	2	18
5	3̸	8̸
– 2	2	9̸
3	0	9

2.

H	T	O
9	2	6
– 6	0	7

3.

H	T	O
7	3	4
– 2	1	8

4.

H	T	O
5	4	8
– 3	3	9

5.

H	T	O
8	6	3
– 2	3	7

6.

H	T	O
6	3	1
– 4	0	2

7.

H	T	O
7	6	5
– 3	2	6

8.

H	T	O
5	6	2
– 3	2	4

Extra Support Some children may forget to change the number of tens when they regroup. Remind them that when they regroup 1 ten as 10 ones, there is one less ten in the tens column.

Teacher Note: Use after Quick Check page 288 to reteach Unit 11, Lesson 5. **(2)**

Name _____

Problem: $2.50
              + 1.25

Problem: $3.89
              − 1.54

Add the pennies.
Add the dimes.
Add the dollars.

Subtract the pennies.
Subtract the dimes.
Subtract the dollars.

$2.	5	0
+ 1.	2	5
$3.	7	5

$2.50
+ 1.25
$3.75

$3.	8	9
− 1.	5	4
$2.	3	5

$3.89
− 1.54
$2.35

Add.

1.	$2.50 + 2.23	2.	$2.10 + 5.00	3.	$6.27 + 2.12	4.	$4.31 + 3.28
5.	$8.56 + 1.03	6.	$4.64 + 2.23	7.	$1.44 + 3.31	8.	$4.27 + 2.72

Subtract.

9.	$4.39 − 2.07	10.	$8.00 − 6.00	11.	$5.31 − 3.21	12.	$9.76 − 2.75
13.	$1.36 − 1.23	14.	$4.96 − 2.42	15.	$8.67 − 4.23	16.	$7.95 − 3.42

Extra Support You may want to discuss with children how problems such as 342 + 123 and $3.42 + $1.23 are alike and how they are different.

Teacher Note: Use after Quick Check page 288 to reteach Unit 11, Lesson 6. **(2)**

How many bicycles in all?
You can skip-count by 2's to find out.

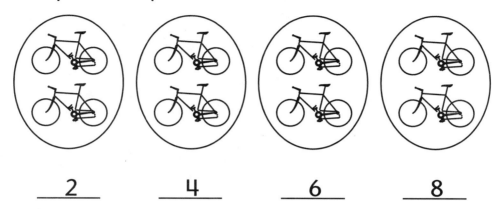

__2__   __4__   __6__   __8__

There are __8__ bicycles in all.

You can use a number line to help you count.

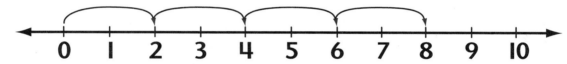

Skip-count to find how many in all.

1.

      _____ in all

2.

            _____ in all

3.

   _____ in all

Extra Support Tell children they may use the number line to help them skip-count.

Teacher Note: Use after Quick Check page 300 to reteach Unit 12, Lesson 1. (2)

How many apples are there in all?
You can add to find out.

2 + 2 + 2 + 2 + 2 + 2 = 12

6 groups of 2 apples   12 apples in all

Complete the addition sentence.

1.

__2__ + _____ + _____ + _____ = _____ in all

2.

_____ + _____ + _____ = _____ in all

3.

_____ + _____ + _____ + _____ + _____ = _____ in all

Extra Support Point out to children that they are adding the same number each time. Each group has an equal number of objects in it. You may wish to have children ring groups of two as they add.

Name _____

How many stars are there in all?
You can **multiply** to find out.

3 rows
2 stars in each row
6 in all

3 groups
2 stars in each group
6 in all

$3 \times 2 = 6$
3 times 2 equals 6.
There are 6 stars in all.

$3 \times 2 = 6$
3 times 2 equals 6.
There are 6 stars in all.

Complete. Find the product.

1.

____2____ groups

____2____ in each group

_____ in all

$2 \times 2 = $ _____

2.

_____ groups

_____ in each group

_____ in all

$4 \times 2 = $ _____

3.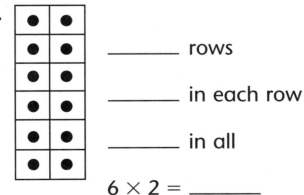

_____ rows

_____ in each row

_____ in all

$6 \times 2 = $ _____

4.

_____ rows

_____ in each row

_____ in all

$5 \times 2 = $ _____

Extra Support Some children may find it helpful to show the problems with counters. Reinforce how the
counters represent the number in each group and the number of groups. You could also have the children arrange
the counters in an array to show equal rows of 2.
Teacher Note: Use after Quick Check page 300 to reteach Unit 12, Lesson 3. (2)

How many hats are there in all?

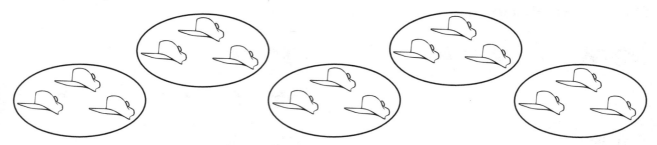

5 groups
3 hats in each group
5 × 3 equals 15.

$$5 \times 3 = 15$$

$$\begin{array}{r} 3 \\ \times 5 \\ \hline 15 \end{array}$$

There are 15 hats in all.

Ring groups of 3. Find the product.

1.

$$2 \times 3 = \underline{\quad 6 \quad}$$

2.

$$3 \times 3 = \underline{\qquad}$$

3.

$$4 \times 3 = \underline{\qquad}$$

4.

$$5 \times 3 = \underline{\qquad}$$

Find the product.

5. $\begin{array}{r} 3 \\ \times 6 \\ \hline \end{array}$

6. $\begin{array}{r} 3 \\ \times 7 \\ \hline \end{array}$

7. $\begin{array}{r} 3 \\ \times 8 \\ \hline \end{array}$

8. $\begin{array}{r} 3 \\ \times 9 \\ \hline \end{array}$

Extra Support Encourage children to use a number line to help them count by 3's if they need help.

Teacher Note: Use after Quick Check page 310 to reteach Unit 12, Lesson 4. **(2)**

How many triangles are there in all?

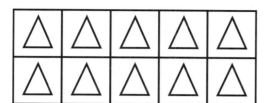

2 rows
5 triangles in each row
10 triangles in all

$2 \times 5 = 10$

$$\begin{array}{r} 5 \\ \times\ 2 \\ \hline 10 \end{array}$$

Find the product.

1.

[image of dot array]

$3 \times 5 = \underline{\ \ 15\ \ }$

2.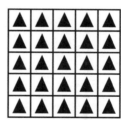

$5 \times 5 = \underline{\hspace{1.5cm}}$

3. $\begin{array}{r} 5 \\ \times\ 5 \\ \hline \end{array}$

4. $\begin{array}{r} 5 \\ \times\ 6 \\ \hline \end{array}$

5. $\begin{array}{r} 5 \\ \times\ 7 \\ \hline \end{array}$

6. $\begin{array}{r} 5 \\ \times\ 8 \\ \hline \end{array}$

7. $\begin{array}{r} 5 \\ \times\ 9 \\ \hline \end{array}$

Extra Support Have children practice counting by 5's using a yardstick or meterstick.

Teacher Note: Use after Quick Check page 310 to reteach Unit 12, Lesson 5. **(2)**

Name_____

You can multiply in any order.

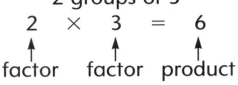

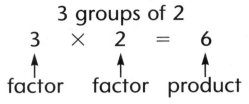

2 groups of 3

2 × 3 = 6

↑   ↑   ↑

factor   factor   product

3 groups of 2

3 × 2 = 6

↑   ↑   ↑

factor   factor   product

2 and 3 are factors. The product is the same.

Write the multiplication sentences.

1.

1 group of 5

__1__ × __5__ = __5__

5 groups of 1

__5__ × __1__ = __5__

2.

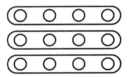

3 groups of 4

_____ × _____ = _____

4 groups of 3

_____ × _____ = _____

3.

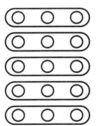

5 groups of 3

_____ × _____ = _____

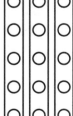

3 groups of 5

_____ × _____ = _____

Extra Support Have children use counters to show each multiplication sentence. Then, ask them to use 12 counters to show a different multiplication sentence for exercise 2.

    Teacher Note: Use after Quick Check page 310 to reteach Unit 12, Lesson 8. **(2)**

Look at the pattern.

· · · · · · · · · · $1 \times 10 = 10$

· · · · · · · · · ·
· · · · · · · · · · $2 \times 10 = 20$

· · · · · · · · · ·
· · · · · · · · · ·
· · · · · · · · · · $3 \times 10 = 30$

· · · · · · · · · ·
· · · · · · · · · ·
· · · · · · · · · ·
· · · · · · · · · · $4 \times 10 = 40$

Write the multiplication sentence.

1.

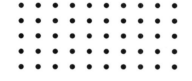

$\underline{\quad 5 \quad} \times \underline{\quad 10 \quad} = \underline{\quad 50 \quad}$

2.

$\underline{\quad\quad} \times \underline{\quad\quad} = \underline{\quad\quad}$

---

3. $\begin{array}{r} 10 \\ \times\, 6 \\ \hline \end{array}$ **4.** $\begin{array}{r} 10 \\ \times\, 0 \\ \hline \end{array}$ **5.** $\begin{array}{r} 10 \\ \times\, 9 \\ \hline \end{array}$ **6.** $\begin{array}{r} 10 \\ \times\, 1 \\ \hline \end{array}$ **7.** $\begin{array}{r} 10 \\ \times\, 8 \\ \hline \end{array}$

Extra Support Have children use a hundred chart to count by 10's.

A **multiplication table** shows the
products for different factors.

Multiply 3 × 2.
Find the 2.
Find the 3.
Find where the factors meet.
6 is the product.

×	②	←factor
0	0	
1	2	
2	4	
③	⑥	←product
4	8	
5	10	

factor→

$3 \times 2 = 6$

Complete the tables.

1.

×	2
0	0
1	2
2	4
3	6
4	
5	
6	
7	
8	
9	
10	

2.

×	5
0	0
1	5
2	10
3	
4	
5	
6	
7	
8	
9	
10	

3.

×	10
0	0
1	10
2	20
3	
4	
5	
6	
7	
8	
9	
10	

Extra Support Some children may need to point to each factor and then say the multiplication sentence aloud.

Teacher Note: Use after Quick Check page 314 to reteach Unit 12, Lesson 10. **(2)**

Favorite Animals

🐴	👤 👤 👤
🐕	👤 👤 👤 👤
🦁	👤 👤 👤 👤 👤

👤 = 2 children

How many children named the horse as their favorite animal?

There are 3 👤 next to the picture of the horse.

Each 👤 stands for 2 children.

Multiply.   3 × 2 = 6   6 children liked the horse best.

How many children liked each animal? Use the picture graph. Complete the number sentence.

1. lion   __5__ × 2 = __10__ children

2. dog   _____ × 2 = _____ children

Solve.

3. Which animal did most children like best? _____

4. How many more children named the lion than the

dog? _____ children

Extra Support Discuss the parts of the graph with children before they begin. Remind them that each figure in the key stands for two children.

Reteach Worksheets

$3 \times \boxed{} = 12$ Find the missing factor.

There are 3 groups of 4.
There are 12 balloons in all.   So $3 \times 4 = 12.$

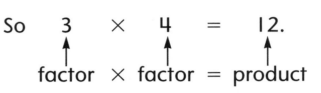

factor × factor = product

Find the missing factor.

1. Ring groups of 5.

   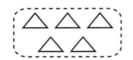 $\boxed{} \times 5 = 10$

---

2. Ring groups of 3.

               $\boxed{} \times 3 = 9$

---

3. How many in each group?

$2 \times \boxed{4} = 8$

---

4. How many in each group?

$2 \times \boxed{} = 6$

Extra Support For children who have difficulty, suggest that they first identify the number of groups (the first factor) and then count the number of objects in each group (the second factor).

Name _____

How many cherries are there in all?__6__

Make 3 groups.   Remember: Each group
has the same number.

How many are in each group?__2__

Count how many in all.
Make equal groups.
Write the number in each group.

1. How many are there in all?__8__

   Make 2 groups.

   How many are in each group?____

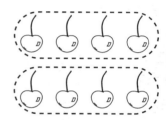

2. How many are there in all?____

   Make 3 groups.

   How many are in each group?____

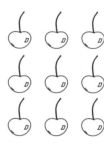

3. How many are there in all?____

   Make 5 groups.

   How many are in each group?____

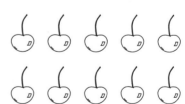

Extra Support Have pairs of children use counters to model the groups for each exercise.

Name _____

Jamal has 6 marbles.
He wants to give them all away.
Each friend will get 2.
How many friends will get marbles?

Subtract to find out.

6	4	2
−2	−2	−2
4	2	0

You subtracted 3 times.
3 friends will get marbles.

Complete.

1. Nita has 12 flowers.
   She wants to put 2 flowers in each vase.
   How many vases does she need?

12	10	8	6	4	2
−2	−2	−2	−2	−2	−2

I subtracted ___6___ times.

Nita needs _____ vases.

2. Erik has a baseball card book.
   Erik has 15 baseball cards.
   He can put 3 cards on each page of his book.
   How many pages will he fill?

15	12	9	6	3
−3	−3	−3	−3	−3

I subtracted _____ times.

Erik will fill _____ pages.

Extra Support Have children use counters to show the repeated subtraction. If they tally each time they subtract, they can keep track of the number of times they subtract.

Teacher Note: Use after Quick Check page 320 to reteach Unit 12, Lesson 14. **(2)**

___7___ apples in all

Ring groups of 2.

How many groups are there?___3___

How many apples are left over?___1___

Complete.

1. _____ in all

Ring groups of 2.

_____ groups

_____ left over

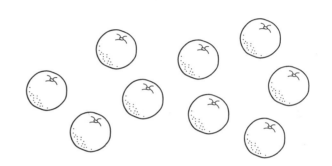

2. _____ in all

Ring groups of 3.

_____ groups

_____ left over

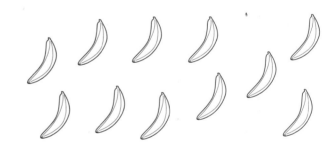

3. _____ in all

Ring groups of 4.

_____ groups

_____ left over

Extra Support Give children 17 counters to make groups of 2, 3, 5, and 10. Ask them to tell how many are left over each time.

Teacher Note: Use after page 322 to reteach Unit 12, Lesson 15. (2)   **165**

You can use a table to solve problems.

Complete the table. Answer the questions.

Each child needs **10** marbles to play Chinese checkers.

children	1	2	3	4	5	6
marbles	10	20	30	40	50	60

1. How many marbles do **5** children need to play? _____ marbles

2. How many children can play with **40** marbles? _____ children

3. How many children can play with **60** marbles? _____ children

Children make teams of **3** for the jump-rope competition.

teams	1	2	3					
children	3	6						

7. How many teams can **18** children make? _____ teams

8. How many children make up **7** teams? _____ children

9. **12** second-graders want to compete.
   How many teams can they make? _____ teams

Extra Support You may wish to fill in the table as a class before having children answer the questions independently.

Teacher Note: Use after Unit 12, Lesson 16. **(2)**

Extension Worksheets

Extension Worksheets

NOTES

Match the domino ends to make a chain.

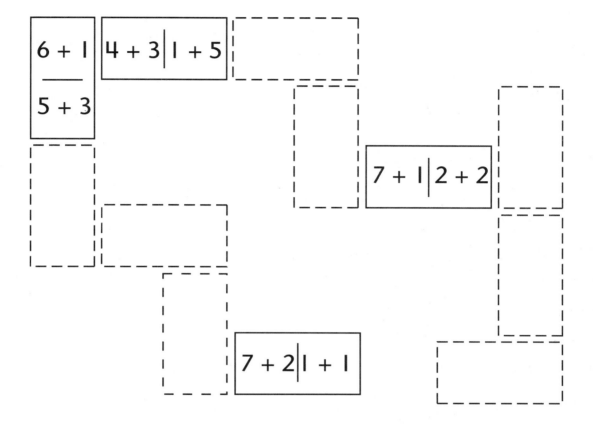

6 + 1	4 + 3	1 + 5

| 5 + 3 |

| 7 + 1 | 2 + 2 |

| 7 + 2 | 1 + 1 |

| 3 + 1 | 1 + 0 | 4 + 4 | 3 + 0 | 5 + 5 | 1 + 8 | 7 + 3 | 2 + 6 |

| 0 + 6 | 9 + 1 | 2 + 7 | 2 + 2 | 3 + 3 | 5 + 4 | 2 + 1 | 4 + 2 |

Write the missing clues.

1.

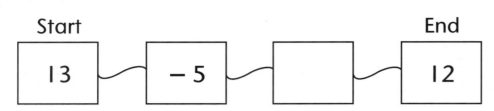

Start — 13 — − 5 — [ ] — End — 12

2.

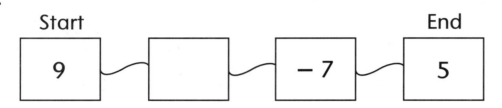

Start — 9 — [ ] — − 7 — End — 5

3.

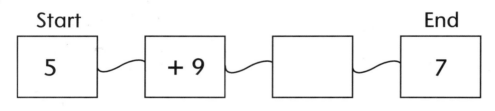

Start — 5 — + 9 — [ ] — End — 7

4.

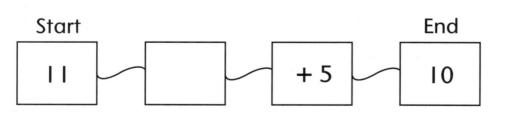

Start — 11 — [ ] — + 5 — End — 10

5.

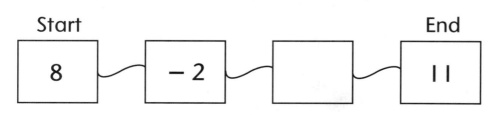

Start — 8 — − 2 — [ ] — End — 11

Teacher Note: Use after Unit 1, Lesson 7. **(2)**

When the number in the ones place is 5, always round up to the next ten.

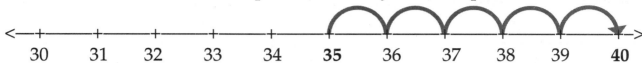

<---+-----+-----+-----+-----+-----+-----+-----+-----+-----+--->
  30   31   32   33   34   **35**   36   37   38   39   **40**

1	2	3	4	5	6	7	8	9	10
11	12	13	14	15	16	17	18	19	20
21	22	23	24	25	26	27	28	29	30
31	32	33	34	35	36	37	38	39	40
41	42	43	44	45	46	47	48	49	50
51	52	53	54	55	56	57	58	59	60
61	62	63	64	65	66	67	68	69	70
71	72	73	74	75	76	77	78	79	80
81	82	83	84	85	86	87	88	89	90
91	92	93	94	95	96	97	98	99	100

Round up to the next ten. Use the hundred chart to help.

1.   45_____   75 _____   25 _____   95 _____

Round to the nearest ten. Remember to round numbers with 5 ones to the next ten.

2.   34 _____   58 _____   92 _____   17 _____

3.   21 _____   77 _____   65 _____   43 _____

4.   15 _____   24 _____   32 _____   78 _____

Teacher Note: Use after Unit 2, Lesson 2. **(2)**

Look at the pattern.

Fill in each ☐.

1.　4,　　7,　　10,　　13, ☐ ,　　19, ☐

2.　16,　　21,　　26,　　31, ☐ ,　　41,　　46

3.　5,　　9,　　13, ☐ ,　　21, ☐ ,　　29

4.　30,　　36,　　42,　　48, ☐ ,　　60, ☐

5.　85,　　80,　　75, ☐ ,　　65, ☐ ,　　55

Teacher Note: Use after Unit 2, Lesson 5. **(2)**

Puzzle 1

Add to find names for 16. Ring the sums of 16.

8 5 6 2 7 3

7 1 8 4 5 2

5 3 4 8 7 1

6 5 9 1 6 4

2 8 4 9 3 7

4 6 3 1 2 9

Puzzle 2

Use + or − to show how to get the answer. You may use each as often as needed.

9 ◯ 5 ◯ 3 = 7

9 ◯ 5 ◯ 3 = 17

9 ◯ 2 ◯ 6 = 5

9 ◯ 2 ◯ 6 = 1

Puzzle 3

Use + and − to show how to get the answer. You may use each as often as needed.

8 ◯ 4 ◯ 7 = 11

8 ◯ 4 ◯ 7 = 5

8 ◯ 3 ◯ 5 = 0

8 ◯ 3 ◯ 5 = 6

Puzzle 4

Add to find names for 14. Ring the sums of 14.

8 6 2 5 7 9

4 7 3 7 8 2

7 1 5 9 1 3

3 6 5 7 9 8

2 8 4 3 1 3

1 6 5 4 7 2

Extension Worksheets

Teacher Note: Use after Unit 3, Lesson 4. **(2)**

These are open figures.  | These are closed figures.

Color inside the closed figures.

1.

Ring the word that describes the figure.

2.   open   closed

3.   open   closed

4.   open   closed

5.   open   closed

Teacher Note: Use after Unit 4, Lesson 2. **(2)**

1								
$\frac{1}{2}$				$\frac{1}{2}$				
$\frac{1}{3}$		$\frac{1}{3}$			$\frac{1}{3}$			
$\frac{1}{4}$		$\frac{1}{4}$		$\frac{1}{4}$		$\frac{1}{4}$		
$\frac{1}{6}$	$\frac{1}{6}$	$\frac{1}{6}$	$\frac{1}{6}$	$\frac{1}{6}$	$\frac{1}{6}$			
$\frac{1}{8}$	$\frac{1}{8}$	$\frac{1}{8}$	$\frac{1}{8}$	$\frac{1}{8}$	$\frac{1}{8}$	$\frac{1}{8}$	$\frac{1}{8}$	
$\frac{1}{9}$	$\frac{1}{9}$	$\frac{1}{9}$	$\frac{1}{9}$	$\frac{1}{9}$	$\frac{1}{9}$	$\frac{1}{9}$	$\frac{1}{9}$	$\frac{1}{9}$

Each fraction strip is one whole divided into different equal parts.

**Use the picture.
Ring the correct answer.**

1. $\frac{1}{4} > \frac{1}{6}$

(true) false

2. $\frac{1}{9} > \frac{1}{2}$

true (false)

3. $\frac{1}{3} < \frac{1}{4}$

true (false)

4. $\frac{1}{8} < \frac{1}{4}$

(true) false

5. $\frac{1}{3} > \frac{1}{9}$

(true) false

6. $\frac{1}{6} > \frac{1}{2}$

true (false)

Write >, <, or =.

7. $\frac{1}{4}$ ◯ $\frac{1}{2}$

8. $\frac{1}{6}$ ◯ $\frac{1}{6}$

9. $\frac{1}{9}$ ◯ $\frac{1}{3}$

Teacher Note: Use after Unit 4, Lesson 6. **(2)**

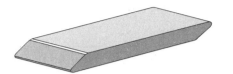

Use the pictured objects as referents.
Estimate which length is longer.
Ring your estimate.

1.   3 erasers   (8 paper clips)

2.   2 markers   7 pennies

3.   5 paper clips   3 markers

4.   6 quarters   5 erasers

5.   4 quarters   4 pennies

Teacher Note: Use after Unit 5, Lesson 1. **(2)**

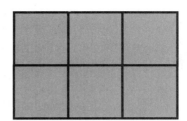

□ is 1 square unit.

The area of the rectangle is 6 square units.

$3 \times 2 = 6$

Write the area.

1.

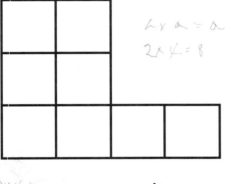

$4 \times a = a$
$2 \times 4 = 8$

_2×4=8_ square units

2.

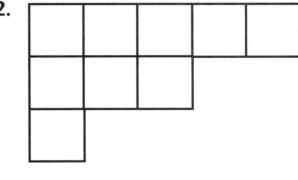

$3 \times 3 = 9$

_3×3=9_ square units

Color to show the number of square units.

3.

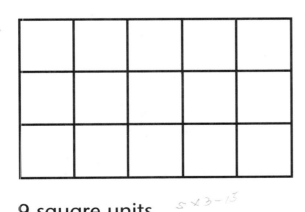

9 square units

$5 \times 3 = 15$

4.

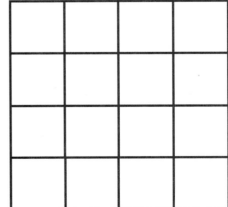

12 square units

$4 \times 4 = 16$

Extension Worksheets

```
←——+—+—+—+—+—+—+—+—+—+—+—+—+—+—+—+—+—+—+—+——→
  20  21  22  23  24  25  26  27  28  29  30  31  32  33  34  35  36  37  38  39 40
```

Round to the nearest ten.

```
  28        28 is nearest 30.    →        | 30 |
 +39        39 is nearest 40.    →      + | 40 |
            Add.          Estimate        | 70 |
```

The sum is about 70.

**Round to the nearest ten.
Add. Write the estimate.**

1. 24 → ☐
   +37 → + ☐

   Estimate ☐

   The sum is about _____.

2. 63 → ☐
   +31 → + ☐

   Estimate ☐

   The sum is about _____.

3. There are 29 children in
   Room A, 31 children in
   Room B, and 27 children in
   Room C. About how many
   children are in all three
   rooms?

   29 → ☐
   31 → ☐
  +27 → + ☐
        ☐

   about _____ children

Teacher Note: Use after Unit 6, Lesson 1. **(2)**

● Use these numbers.   1   3   6   7

Write all the 2-digit numbers you can make.
Each number must have 2 different digits.

13 _____   _____   _____

_____   _____   _____

_____   _____   _____

_____   _____   _____

Use the numbers from above.

1. Write the greatest number. _____

2. Write the least number. _____

3. What is their sum?

_____ + _____ = _____

Use the numbers from above.
Make up your own addition exercises.

4. 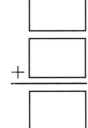   **5.** 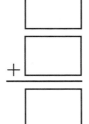   **6.** 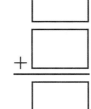   **7.**

Teacher Note: Use after Unit 6, Lesson 8. **(2)**

Use only the digits 1, 2, 3, 4.

Put one digit in each to get the answer.

1.

```
        □
    2
+   □    5
───────────
    6    8
```

Try 3 and 4.

2.

```
    □
         7
+   2    □
───────────
    6    9
```

3.

```
        □
    6
+   □    3
───────────
    9    5
```

4.

```
    4    5
+   □    □
───────────
    8    8
```

5.

```
    □
         3
+   4    □
───────────
    7    5
```

6.

```
        □
    7
+   □    4
───────────
    9    6
```

180

Teacher Note: Use after Unit 6, Lesson 8. **(2)**

```
 ←——┼—┼—┼—┼—┼—┼—┼—┼—┼—┼—┼—┼—┼—┼—┼—┼—┼—┼—┼—┼—→
    30  31  32  33  34  35  36  37  38  39  40  41  42  43  44  45  46  47  48  49  50
```

Round to the nearest ten.

47   47 is nearest 50.   →   ☐ 50

−39   39 is nearest 40.   →   − ☐ 40

          Subtract.   Estimate   ☐ 10

The difference is about 10.

Round to the nearest ten.
Subtract. Write the estimate.

1.   42 → ☐

   −33 → − ☐

Estimate ☐

The difference is about _____.

2.   57 → ☐

   −18 → − ☐

Estimate ☐

The difference is about _____.

Ring the estimate.

3. At the fish store, tank 1 has 58 fish. Tank 2 has 27 fish. How many more fish are in tank 1?

about 20   about 30

4. Carol has 78¢. She buys a yo-yo for 49¢. About how much money does she have left?

about 30¢   about 40¢

Extension Worksheets

Make names for 40.

22 + 18	78 − 38
5 + 5 + 30	

Teacher Note: Use after Unit 7, Lesson 12. **(2)**

You can write number sentences to help you solve problems.

1. Rita has 27 fish. She gives 13 fish to her friend. Then, she buys 8 more fish. How many fish does she have now?

Answer: _____ fish

Step 1: 27 - 13 =

$$\begin{array}{r} 27 \\ -13 \\ \hline 14 \end{array}$$ fish

Step 2: 14 + 8 =

$$\begin{array}{r} 14 \\ +\ 8 \\ \hline 22 \end{array}$$ fish

2. Carlos catches 15 sunfish. D.J. catches 21 bass. Maria catches 27 pike. They give away 14 of their fish. How many fish do they have left?

Answer: _____ fish

Step 1: 15 + 21 + 27 =

Step 2:

3. Kendra has 99¢ to spend at the fish store. She picks out lures that cost 15¢, 27¢, and 42¢. How much change will she get back?

Answer: _____ ¢

Does she have enough money left to buy a lure that costs 1 dime and 3 pennies?

Answer: _____

Teacher Note: Use after Unit 7, Lesson 14. **(2)**

Name _____

Show the beginning and ending times. Solve.

1. Riaz arrives at Ryan's house at 10:00 A.M. He leaves at 2:00 P.M. How long does he stay at Ryan's house?

Answer: _____ hours

2. Each lunch period is 30 minutes long. The first lunch period starts at 11:30 A.M. There are three lunch periods each day. What time do the last children finish eating lunch?

Answer: _____

3. Tori rakes leaves for 4 hours. If she finishes at 3:30 P.M., what time did she start raking?

Answer: _____

4. The bus leaves at 9:00 A.M. It stops every 45 minutes. It makes a total of 4 stops. What time does the bus make the last stop?

Answer: _____

Teacher Note: Use after Unit 8, Lesson 6. **(2)**

APRIL
S	M	T	W	T	F	S
		1	2	3	4
5	6	7	8	9	10	11
12	13	14	15	16	17	18
19	20	21	22	23	24	25
26	27	28	29	30		

60 seconds = 1 minute
60 minutes = 1 hour
24 hours = 1 day
7 days = 1 week

Ring the one that is longer.

1. (3 weeks) or 18 days

2. 27 days or 3 weeks

3. 100 seconds or 2 minutes

4. 3 minutes or 300 seconds

5. 30 hours or 1 day

6. 2 days or 35 hours

7. 2 hours or 70 minutes

8. 150 minutes or 3 hours

Solve.

9. Which is longer, 50 hours or 2 days? Why?

_____

_____

Extension Worksheets

Teacher Note: Use after Unit 8, Lesson 8. **(2)**

Read the clues.
Paste the coins in the banks.

1.

Put in 3 coins.
Make 31¢
in all.

31¢

2.

Put in 4 coins.
Make 16¢
in all.

16¢

3.

Put in 4 coins.
Make 17¢
in all.

17¢

4.

Put in 3 coins.
Make 27¢
in all.

27¢

Teacher Note: Use after Unit 8, Lesson 11. **(2)**

Color to solve. You need yellow and red crayons.

1. A rug has 4 parts. If you color each part either yellow or red, how many different ways can you color the rug?

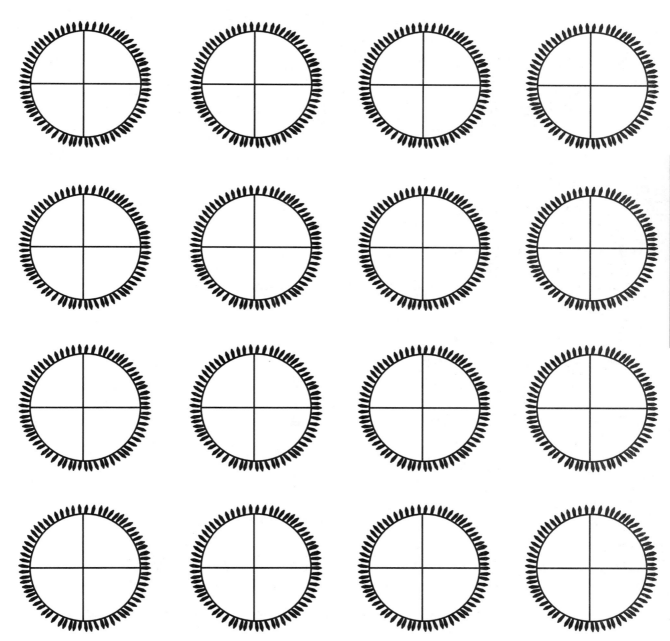

Extension Worksheets

What are the chances?

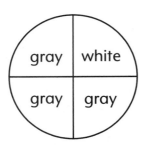

stopping on white

I chance in ___4___

stopping on gray

3 chances in ___4___

1. Are you more likely to stop on gray or white? Why?

_____

_____

What are the chances?

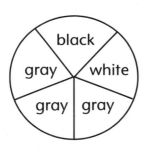

2. stopping on white

___1___ chance in ___5___

3. stopping on black

_____ chance in _____

4. stopping on gray

_____ chances in _____

5. Are you more likely to stop on black or gray? Why?

_____

6. Will you stop on red? Why or why not?

_____

Teacher Note: Use after Unit 9, Lesson 6. **(2)**

| 100 pennies = $1.00 | 20 nickels = $1.00 |
| 10 dimes = $1.00 | 4 quarters = $1.00 |

Solve.

1. How many pennies equal $1.32?

   _____ pennies

2. How many pennies equal $2.12?

   _____ pennies

3. How many dimes equal $1.80?

   _____ dimes

4. How many dimes equal $3.50?

   _____ dimes

5. How many nickels equal $1.35?

   _____ nickels

6. How many nickels equal $3.60?

   _____ nickels

7. How many quarters equal $4.00?

   _____ quarters

8. How many quarters equal $6.50?

   _____ quarters

Extension Worksheets

Teacher Note: Use after Unit 10, Lesson 12. **(2)**

189

The sum of the digits in 146 equals 11.

$$1 + 4 + 6 = 11$$

The sum of the digits in 232 = ?

$$2 + 3 + 2 = 7$$

Find the sum of the digits.

1. 137 = _____

2. 281 = _____

3. 346 = _____

4. 467 = _____

5. 544 = _____

6. 892 = _____

Solve.

7. The sum of the digits in 288 equals 18.
Write another 3-digit number whose digits add up to 18.

_____

Teacher Note: Use after Unit 11, Lesson 1. **(2)**

Skip-count by 9's.

1. _____, __18__, _____, _____, _____,

_____54_____, _____, __72__, _____, __90__

....

Solve.

2. What is the sum of the digits in 18? _____

3. What is the sum of the digits in 27? _____

4. What is the sum of the digits in 36? _____

5. What pattern do you see? _____

_____

....

6. **Skip-count by 25's.**

_____, __50__, _____, _____, _____,

_____, __175__, _____, __225__, _____,

_____, _____, _____, _____, _____,

__400__, _____, __450__, _____, _____

Teacher Note: Use after Unit 12, Lesson 1. **(2)**

Complete the facts.
Use the products to solve the riddle.

1.

2 × 1 =	B
2 × 2 =	C
2 × 3 =	P
2 × 4 =	D
2 × 5 =	T
2 × 6 =	F
2 × 7 =	G
2 × 8 =	H
2 × 9 =	I
2 × 10 =	E

2.

5 × 1 =	A
5 × 2 =	T
5 × 3 =	B
5 × 4 =	E
5 × 5 =	M
5 × 6 =	R
5 × 7 =	C
5 × 8 =	D
5 × 9 =	U
5 × 10 =	F

3.

10 × 1 =	T
10 × 2 =	E
10 × 3 =	R
10 × 4 =	B
10 × 5 =	C
10 × 6 =	D
10 × 7 =	G
10 × 8 =	I
10 × 9 =	E
10 × 10 =	J

4. Riddle: What goes up and down but doesn't move?

____ ____ ____
10   16   90

____ ____ ____ ____ ____ ____ ____ ____ ____ ____ ____
10   20   25   6   20   30   5   10   45   30   20

Teacher Note: Use after Unit 12, Lesson 10. **(2)**

Solve.

Wanda plants 30 flower plants.
She puts 10 plants in each row.
How may rows does she plant?

X X X X X X X X X X

X X X X X X X X X X

___3___ rows

X X X X X X X X X X

What multiplication sentence shows the problem?

$10 \times \boxed{3} = 30$

Solve.

1. What if Wanda plants 3 flower plants in each row? How many rows does she plant?

   Draw a picture to solve.

   _____ rows

   $3 \times \boxed{} = 30$

2. What if Wanda plants 5 flower plants in each row? How many rows does she plant?

   Draw a picture to solve.

   _____ rows

   $5 \times \boxed{} = 30$

Extension Worksheets

Teacher Note: Use after Unit 12, Lesson 12. **(2)**

Teaching Resources

Teaching Resources

Month _____

Sunday	Monday	Tuesday	Wednesday	Thursday	Friday	Saturday

Teaching Resources

Name _____

Number line 1: 0 1 2 3 4 5 6 7 8 9 10 11 12

Number line 2: 0 1 2 3 4 5 6 7 8 9 10 11 12

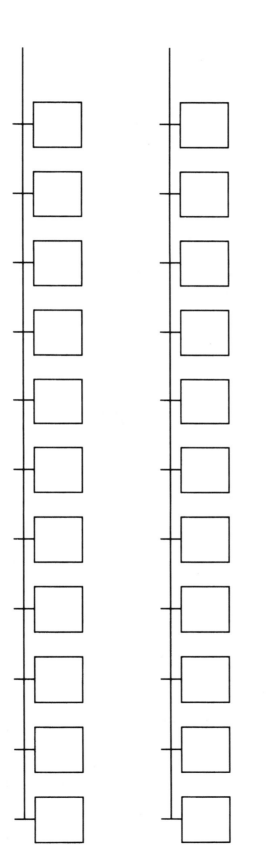
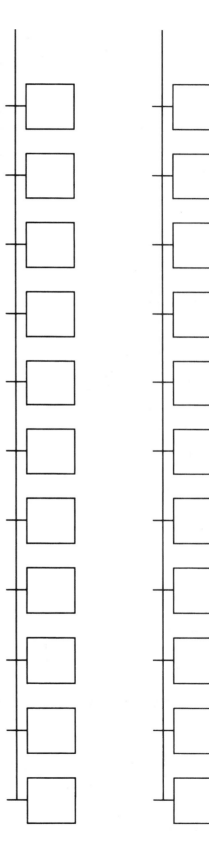

Teaching Resources

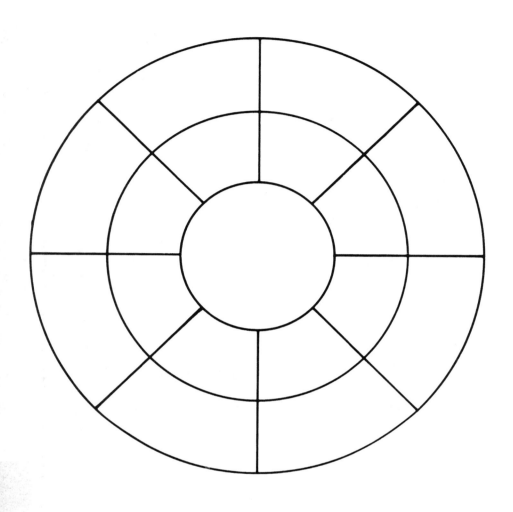

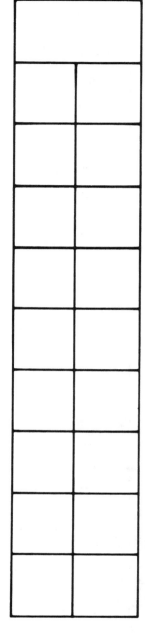

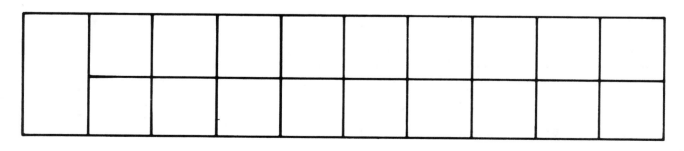

Ones

Tens

Hundreds	Tens	Ones

1	2	3	4	5	6	7	8	9	10
11	12	13	14	15	16	17	18	19	20
21	22	23	24	25	26	27	28	29	30
31	32	33	34	35	36	37	38	39	40
41	42	43	44	45	46	47	48	49	50
51	52	53	54	55	56	57	58	59	60
61	62	63	64	65	66	67	68	69	70
71	72	73	74	75	76	77	78	79	80
81	82	83	84	85	86	87	88	89	90
91	92	93	94	95	96	97	98	99	100

Teaching Resources

Teaching Resources

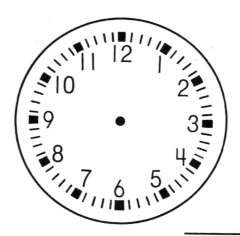

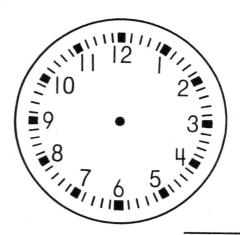

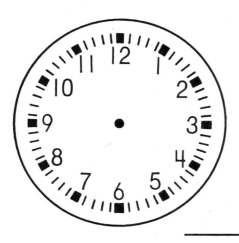

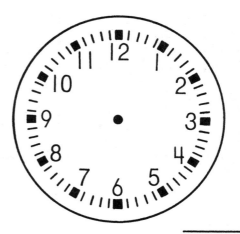

Teaching Resources

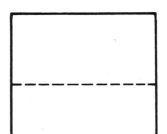
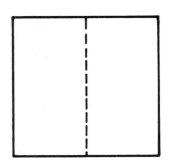
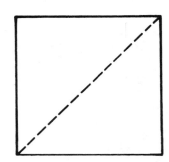

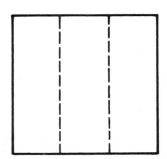
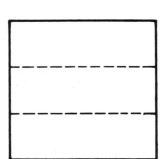
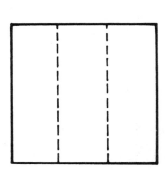

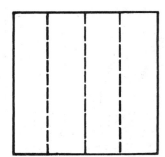
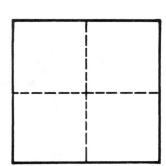
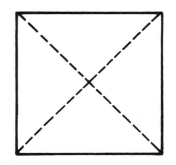

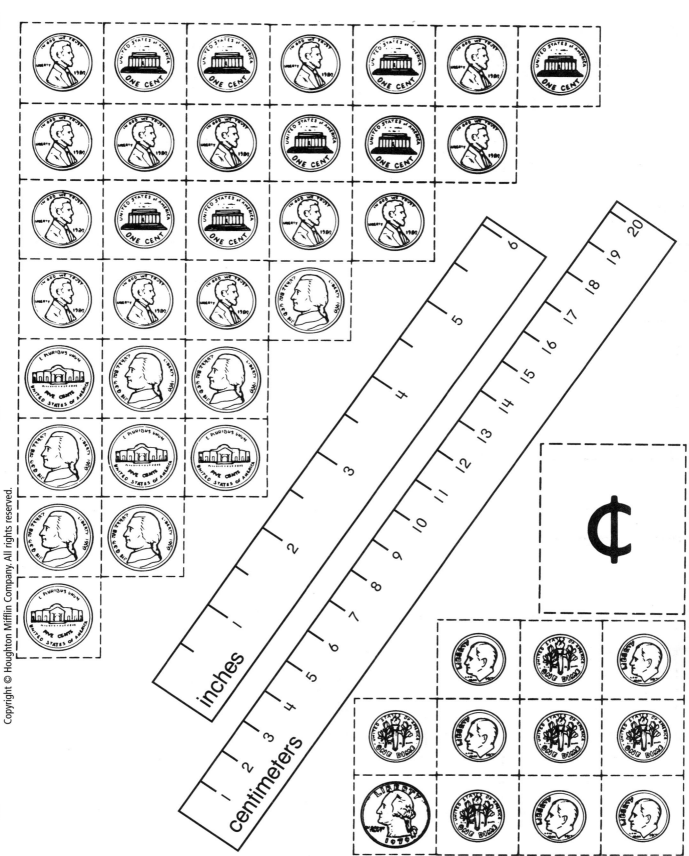

Teaching Resources

20							
19							
18							
17							
16							
15							
14							
13							
12							
11							
10							
9							
8							
7							
6							
5							
4							
3							
2							
1							
0							

Whole

Part	Part

Teaching Resources

Spin a number. Model it with counters. Record it on the first line.

Spin another number. Model it and record it on the second line.

Decide whether one number is greater or if the numbers are equal. Record <, >, or = in the circle.

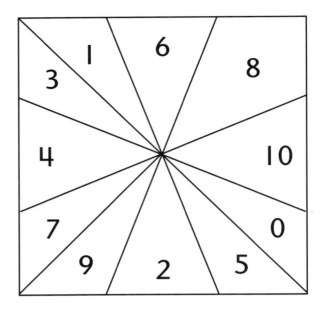

1. ____ ◯ ____   ____ ◯ ____

2. ____ ◯ ____   ____ ◯ ____

3. ____ ◯ ____   ____ ◯ ____

4. ____ ◯ ____   ____ ◯ ____

5. ____ ◯ ____   ____ ◯ ____

6. ____ ◯ ____   ____ ◯ ____

1. ____ tens ____ ones = _____

2. ____ tens ____ ones = _____

3. ____ tens ____ ones = _____

4. ____ tens ____ ones = _____

5. ____ tens ____ ones = _____

6. ____ tens ____ ones = _____

7. ____ tens ____ ones = _____

8. ____ tens ____ ones = _____

9. ____ tens ____ ones = _____

10. ____ tens ____ ones = _____

Name_____

 Use your pencil and a paper clip to spin a number. Make a connecting cube train of one color to show it. Spin another number and make a train of another color to show it. Tell your group what fact family the trains show. Write the fact family. Repeat until you have 6 different fact families.

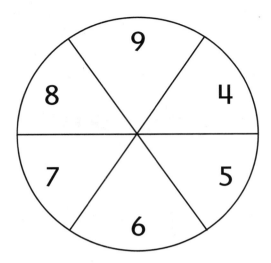

Functions
+0

add 4

double it

−4

subtract 3

−5

subtract 3

+1

−0

+3

add 5

For each chart, toss a counter into the box. Write the function nearest your counter in the blank at the top of the chart. Complete each chart.

1. _____

6	
4	
8	
7	
9	

2. _____

7	
4	
6	
9	
8	

3. _____

10	
6	
5	
9	
7	

4. _____

4	
6	
8	
10	
12	

5. _____

5	
7	
9	
11	
13	

6. _____

Teaching Resources

Make a shape. Change it. Record sides, corners, and names.

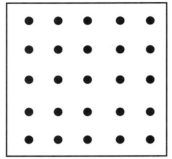 sides

_____

corners

_____

_____

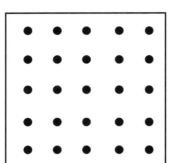 sides

_____

corners

_____

_____

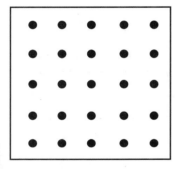 sides

_____

corners

_____

_____

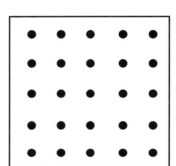 sides

_____

corners

_____

_____

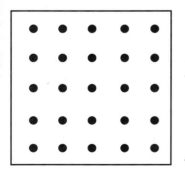 sides

_____

corners

_____

_____

sides

_____

corners

_____

_____

Make symmetrical designs. Record your work.

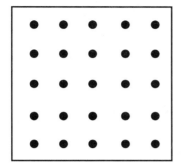
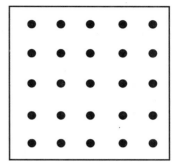

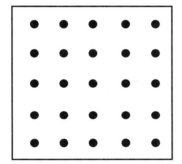
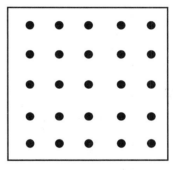

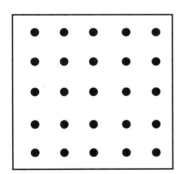
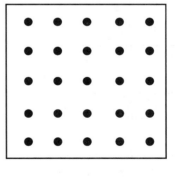

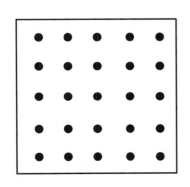
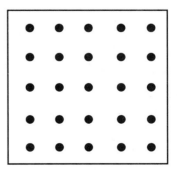

Teaching Resources

Model unit fractions. Ring the fraction name.

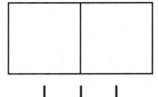

$\dfrac{1}{2}$ $\dfrac{1}{3}$ $\dfrac{1}{4}$

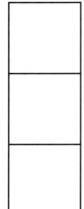

$\dfrac{1}{4}$ $\dfrac{1}{5}$ $\dfrac{1}{6}$

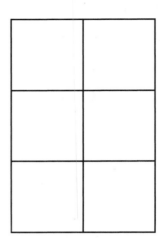

$\dfrac{1}{6}$ $\dfrac{1}{3}$ $\dfrac{1}{2}$

$\dfrac{1}{8}$ $\dfrac{1}{10}$ $\dfrac{1}{12}$

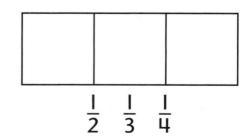

$\dfrac{1}{12}$ $\dfrac{1}{2}$ $\dfrac{1}{10}$

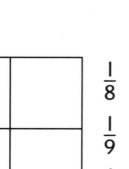

$\dfrac{1}{8}$

$\dfrac{1}{9}$

$\dfrac{1}{10}$

$\dfrac{1}{2}$ $\dfrac{1}{3}$ $\dfrac{1}{4}$

Choose and draw objects. Record estimates and measurements.

Object	Estimate			Measurement		
I. (pencil)	less than a pound	about a pound	more than a pound	less than a pound	about a pound	more than a pound
2.	less than a pound	about a pound	more than a pound	less than a pound	about a pound	more than a pound
3.	less than a pound	about a pound	more than a pound	less than a pound	about a pound	more than a pound
4.	less than a pound	about a pound	more than a pound	less than a pound	about a pound	more than a pound
5.	less than a kilogram	about a kilogram	more than a kilogram	less than a kilogram	about a kilogram	more than a kilogram
6.	less than a kilogram	about a kilogram	more than a kilogram	less than a kilogram	about a kilogram	more than a kilogram
7.	less than a kilogram	about a kilogram	more than a kilogram	less than a kilogram	about a kilogram	more than a kilogram
8.	less than a kilogram	about a kilogram	more than a kilogram	less than a kilogram	about a kilogram	more than a kilogram

Teaching Resources

Name _____

Start with: **Add:**

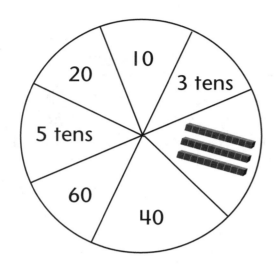

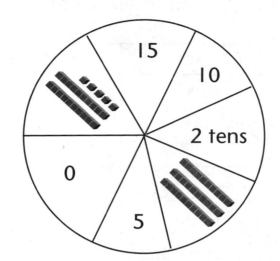

 **Spin. Record what you spin. Solve.**

1. _____ + _____ = _____

2. _____ + _____ = _____

3. _____ + _____ = _____

4. _____ + _____ = _____

5. _____ + _____ = _____

220

Work in groups of 4 or 5. Fill in names and numbers
of counters. Solve the problems.

name	counters

1. How many more counters does _____ have than _____?

   Answer _____

2. How many more counters does _____ have than _____?

   Answer _____

Use a new number of counters for each person.
Fill in the table. Fill in names and solve.

name	counters

3. How many more counters does _____ have than _____?

   Answer _____

4. How many more counters does _____ have than _____?

   Answer _____

Teaching Resources

Show the time by drawing the hands.

1.

9:15

2.

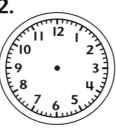

3:05

3.

12:20

4.

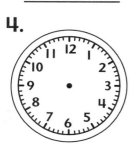

7:50

5.

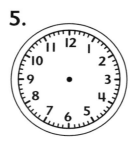

1:25

6.

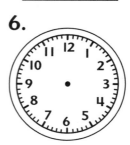

4:10

Write the time.

7.

_____

8.

_____

9.

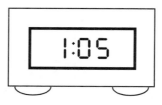

1:05

_____

10.

_____

11.

_____

12.

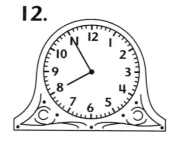

_____

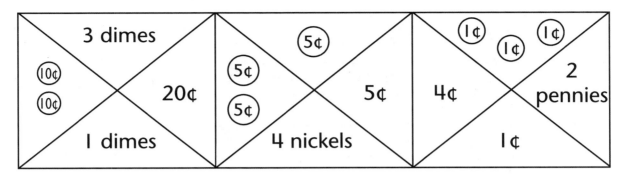

 **Spin. Draw the coins. Count and write the total.**

_____

_____ ¢

_____

_____ ¢

_____

_____ ¢

_____

_____ ¢

_____

_____ ¢

Teaching Resources

chart title _____

	tally	number
Team 1		
Team 2		
Team 3		
Team 4		

graph title _____

Team 4										
Team 3										
Team 2										
Team 1										

0   1   2   3   4   5   6   7   8   9   10

chart title _____

	tally	number
Team 1		
Team 2		
Team 3		
Team 4		

graph title _____

Team 4										
Team 3										
Team 2										
Team 1										

Graph

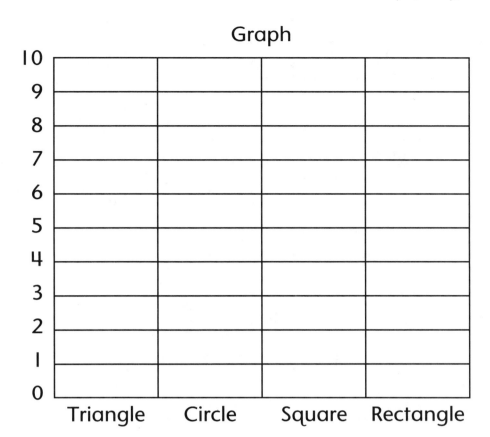

| | Triangle | Circle | Square | Rectangle |

Tally

Line Plot

Teaching Resources

100	110	120	130	140	150	160	170	180	190
101	111	121	131	141	151	161	171	181	191
102	112	122	132	142	152	162	172	182	192
103	113	123	133	143	153	163	173	183	193
104	114	124	134	144	154	164	174	184	194
105	115	125	135	145	155	165	175	185	195
106	116	126	136	146	156	166	176	186	196
107	117	127	137	147	157	167	177	187	197
108	118	128	138	148	158	168	178	188	198
109	119	129	139	149	159	169	179	189	199
									200

200	210	220	230	240	250	260	270	280	290
201	211	221	231	241	251	261	271	281	291
202	212	222	232	242	252	262	272	282	292
203	213	223	233	243	253	263	273	283	293
204	214	224	234	244	254	264	274	284	294
205	215	225	235	245	255	265	275	285	295
206	216	226	236	246	256	266	276	286	296
207	217	227	237	247	257	267	277	287	297
208	218	228	238	248	258	268	278	288	298
209	219	229	239	249	259	269	279	289	299
									300

Teaching Resources

300	310	320	330	340	350	360	370	380	390
301	311	321	331	341	351	361	371	381	391
302	312	322	332	342	352	362	372	382	392
303	313	323	333	343	353	363	373	383	393
304	314	324	334	344	354	364	374	384	394
305	315	325	335	345	355	365	375	385	395
306	316	326	336	346	356	366	376	386	396
307	317	327	337	347	357	367	377	387	397
308	318	328	338	348	358	368	378	388	398
309	319	329	339	349	359	369	379	389	399
									400

Teaching Resource 33

Number Chart 400–500

400	410	420	430	440	450	460	470	480	490
401	411	421	431	441	451	461	471	481	491
402	412	422	432	442	452	462	472	482	492
403	413	423	433	443	453	463	473	483	493
404	414	424	434	444	454	464	474	484	494
405	415	425	435	445	455	465	475	485	495
406	416	426	436	446	456	466	476	486	496
407	417	427	437	447	457	467	477	487	497
408	418	428	438	448	458	468	478	488	498
409	419	429	439	449	459	469	479	489	499
									500

Teaching Resources

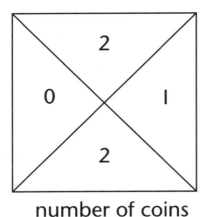

number of coins

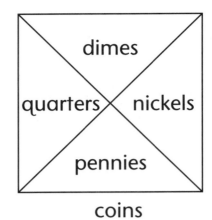

coins

Spin. Draw and count coins, Write the amount 2 ways.

1.

_____¢ $._____

2.

_____¢ $._____

3.

_____¢ $._____

4.

_____¢ $._____

5.

_____¢ $._____

6.

_____¢ $._____

7.

_____¢ $._____

Use your tiles to make arrays to find the products. Record each array.

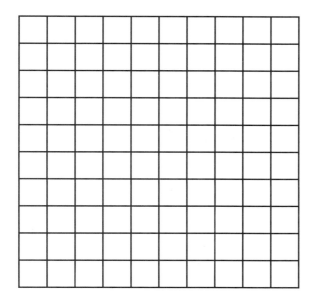

$$2 \times 6 = 12$$

$$6 \times 2 = 12$$

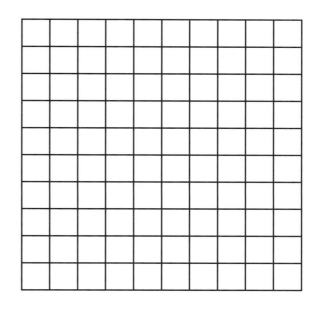

$$3 \times 4 = \underline{\hspace{1.5cm}}$$

$$4 \times 3 = \underline{\hspace{1.5cm}}$$

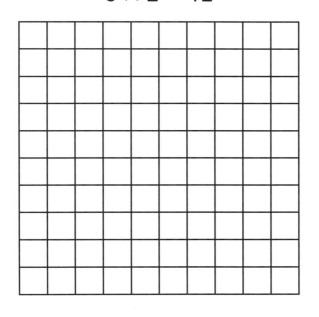

$$5 \times 3 = \underline{\hspace{1.5cm}}$$

$$\underline{\hspace{1.5cm}} \times \underline{\hspace{1.5cm}} = \underline{\hspace{1.5cm}}$$

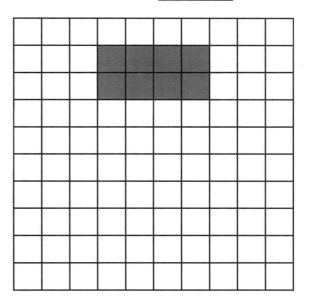

$$\underline{\hspace{1.5cm}} \times \underline{\hspace{1.5cm}} = \underline{\hspace{1.5cm}}$$

$$\underline{\hspace{1.5cm}} \times \underline{\hspace{1.5cm}} = \underline{\hspace{1.5cm}}$$

Teaching Resources

Make equal groups. Fill in the chart. Complete the number sentence.

number of counters	number of groups	number of counters in each group
12	4	
12	6	
12	12	
16	2	
16	4	
16	8	
16	16	
24	2	
24	3	
24	4	
24	6	
24	8	

12 = 4 groups of _____

12 = 6 groups of _____

12 = 12 groups of _____

16 = 2 groups of _____

16 = 4 groups of _____

16 = 8 groups of _____

16 = 16 groups of _____

24 = 2 groups of _____

24 = 3 groups of _____

24 = 4 groups of _____

24 = 6 groups of _____

24 = 8 groups of _____

Name_____

Cut out and use the cards on this page to help your child practice addition facts.

6 +6	7 +4	1 +8	3 +8	6 +4
7 +5	4 +5	4 +8	9 +1	2 +9
9 +3	8 +3	3 +5	5 +7	7 +2
6 +3	8 +4	5 +6	7 +0	3 +9
8 +2	9 +2	4 +3	4 +7	6 +5

Family Note:
• Cut out the flash cards and the puppy card. Place the flash cards in rows and columns facing up.
• Have your child cover his or her eyes while you put the puppy card under a flash card.
• Tell your child the sum of the numbers under which the "puppy" is hidden.
• Ask your child to check all the possible hiding places.
• After the puppy is discovered, the child turns over the flash card under which the puppy was hidden.
• Repeat this sequence until all cards have been turned over.

Family Project Unit 1 (2)

Family Projects

Use a jar of beans and the activity below to help your child practice estimation.

Think!

Do you think there are more or fewer than 25 beans?

Do you think there are more or fewer than 50 beans?

Write.

estimate _____

actual number _____

✂ —

Family Note:
- Put 25–100 beans in a clear jar.
- Place the jar of beans in front of your child.
- Discuss the questions above and ask your child to estimate how many beans are in the jar.
- Have your child select an estimate and write it in the space above.
- Help your child count the beans, counting groups of ten and 1, 2, 3, 4,. . .more.
  EXAMPLE: *Count, 10, 20, and 1,2, 3 more...23!*
- Write the actual number in the space above.
- Have your child compare the number of beans to his or her estimate.
- Remind your child that estimation takes practice.
- This activity can be repeated with different-size containers and objects.

Cut out and use the cards on this page and page 236 to help your child practice addition and subtraction facts.

7 +6	9 +6	8 +5	9 +9	0 +7
5 +9	8 +6	8 +8	7 +8	9 +7
5 +8	9 +8	9 +5	0 +9	7 +7
7 +9	6 +7	4 +9	6 +8	6 +9
8 +9	9 +4	8 +0	8 +7	3 +7

✂ -

Family Note:
- Cut out the flash cards.
- Show one to your child.
- Ask your child to give the sum or difference and to name the related addition and subtraction facts.

Family Projects

13 -9	14 -7	17 -9	9 -9	15 -9
12 -9	7 -0	12 -8	12 -6	11 -3
8 -8	9 -5	16 -7	18 -9	14 -6
13 -5	13 -7	11 -5	15 -8	14 -8
12 -7	9 -4	14 -5	13 -4	15 -7
16 -9	10 -5	9 -6	15 -6	16 -8
10 -6	14 -9	13 -9		

Use the pictures below to help your child identify and list solid figures found at home.

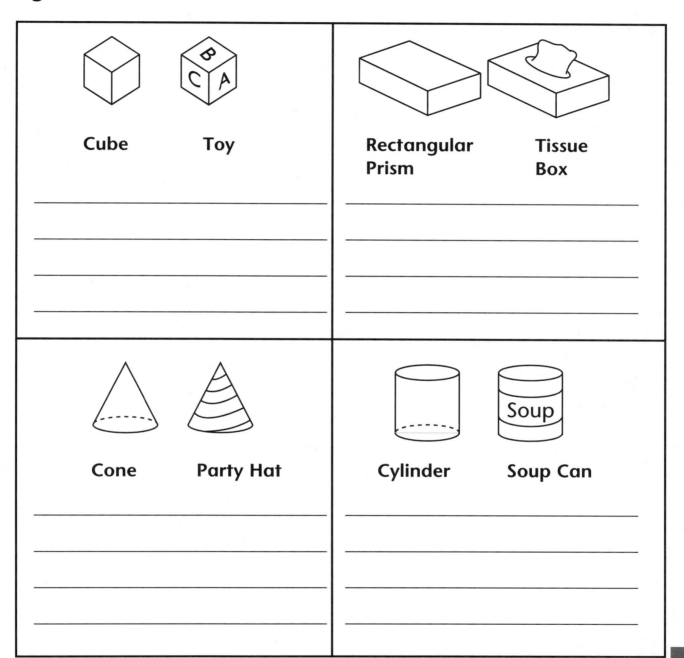

Cube	Toy

_____
_____
_____
_____

Rectangular Prism	Tissue Box

_____
_____
_____
_____

Cone	Party Hat

_____
_____
_____
_____

Cylinder	Soup Can

_____
_____
_____
_____

✂ –

Family Note:
• Discuss the solid figures and household objects shown above. Help your child look around your home for items that match each figure.
• Help your child label each item (on a self-stick note) with the name of the figure to which it corresponds. Record the name of the item in the chart above.

Family Projects

Use a ruler, household objects, and the activity below to help your child practice using a ruler.

Measure and write.

Item	Measurement
_____	_____ inches
_____	_____ inches
_____	_____ inches
_____	_____ inches
_____	_____ inches
_____	_____ inches
_____	_____ inches
_____	_____ inches
_____	_____ foot
_____	_____ foot
_____	_____ foot
_____	_____ foot

✂ - ✂ - - -

Family Note:
- Gather a ruler, a pencil, and some objects that are 1, 4, 6, 8, and 10 inches long. Gather other objects that are 12 inches long. (If you prefer, make paper strips of different lengths.)
- Ask your child to look at the ruler and show you the 6-inch mark. Have him or her look at the objects and pick one that is 6 inches long.
- Ask your child to measure the object. Help him or her record the measurement above.
- Check that your child aligns the ruler correctly when measuring.
- When this page is finished, you may wish to help your child measure and record his or her height, arm span, wrist, and foot. He or she can record the measurements on a separate sheet labeled "Measuring Me."

● **Help your child recognize the patterns in each row of exercises.**

We know:	So,	Then,	Solve.	Solve.
8 + 7 = 15	18 + 7 = 25	28 + 7 = 35	38 + 7= ___	48 + 7 = ___

6 + 7 = 13	16 + 7 = 23	26 + 7 = 33	36 + 7 = ___	46 + 7 = ___

5 + 9 = 14	15 + 9 = 24	25 + 9 = 34	35 + 9 = ___	45 + 9 = ___

3 + 7 = 10	13 + 7 = 20	23 + 7 = 30	33 + 7 = ___	43 + 7 = ___

8 + 4 = 12	18 + 4 = 22	28 + 4 = 32	38 + 4 = ___	48 + 4 = ___

3 + 8 = 11	13 + 8 = 21	23 + 8 = 31	33 + 8 = ___	43 + 8 = ___

✂ -

Family Note:
• Discuss the first example above.
• Talk with your child about the number pattern in the example.
• Help your child complete each row.
• Ask him or her to describe the patterns.
• You may wish to use a separate sheet to create new sets of addition sentences.
Answers:
38 + 7 = 45, 48 + 7 = 55; 36 + 7 = 43, 46 + 7 = 53; 35 + 9 = 44, 45 + 9 = 54;
33 + 7 = 40, 43 + 7 = 50; 38 + 4 = 42, 48 + 4 = 52; 33 + 8 = 41, 43 + 8 = 51

Family Projects

Help your child recognize the patterns in each row of exercises.

We know:	So,	Then,	Solve.	Solve.
$18 - 9 = 9$	$28 - 9 = 19$	$28 - 9 = 19$	$38 - 9 = 29$	$48 - 9 =$ ___

$16 - 7 = 9$	$26 - 7 = 19$	$36 - 7 = 29$	$46 - 7 =$ ___	$56 - 7 =$ ___

$14 - 6 = 8$	$24 - 6 = 18$	$34 - 6 = 28$	$44 - 6 =$ ___	$54 - 6 =$ ___

$12 - 7 = 5$	$22 - 7 = 15$	$32 - 7 = 25$	$42 - 7 =$ ___	$52 - 7 =$ ___

$11 - 4 = 7$	$21 - 4 = 17$	$31 - 4 = 27$	$41 - 4 =$ ___	$51 - 4 =$ ___

$15 - 8 = 7$	$25 - 8 = 17$	$35 - 8 = 27$	$45 - 8 =$ ___	$55 - 8 =$ ___

✂ -

Family Note:
- Talk with your child about the number pattern in the the first row above.
- Help your child complete each row. Ask him or her to describe the patterns.
- You may wish to use a separate sheet to create new sets of subtraction sentences.

Answers:
$48 - 9 = 39$; $46 - 7 = 39$, $56 - 7 = 49$: $44 - 6 = 38$, $54 - 6 = 48$; $42 - 7 = 35$, $52 - 7 = 45$;
$41 - 4 = 37$, $51 - 4 = 47$; $45 - 8 = 33$, $55 - 8 = 43$

Help your child make a clock for practicing telling time.

How to Make a Clock

Step 1: Use a marker to write the numbers on the paper plate. Write in order and in the correct position: 12, 6, 9, and 3. Fill in the rest of the numbers, taking care to space them evenly.

Step 2: Cut out of poster board, a minute and hour hand. Make a hole in each clock hand and in the paper plate. To fasten the hands to the clock face, push the paper fastener through the paper plate and both hands. Press the paper fastener down on the back of the plate to secure it.

Help your child show these times on the clock.

12:30
3:15
6:00
8:45
11:05
1:10
4:25
7:55
10:10

✂ ---

Family Note:
- Gather a paper plate, a paper fastener, poster board, and scissors.
- Help your child make a clock by following the directions above.
- When the clock is complete, ask your child to move the hands on the clock to show different times.

Family Projects

Help your child read the tally chart and bar graph.

Baskets Made in a Game		
Name	**Tally**	**Total**
David	𝍸 𝍸 𝍸	15
Jorge	𝍸 𝍸 𝍸 𝍸 𝍸	25
Mario	𝍸 𝍸	10
Chang	𝍸 𝍸 𝍸 𝍸	20

Baskets Made in a Game

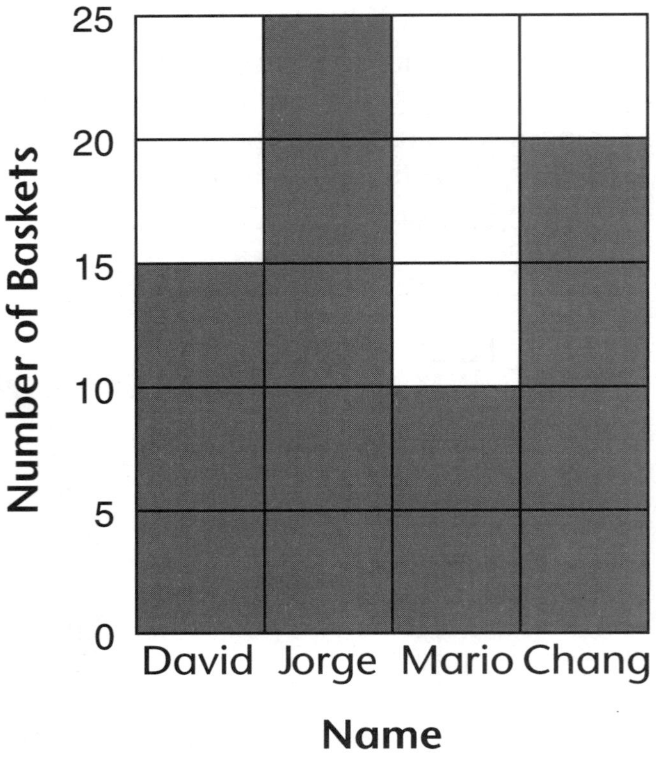

Family Note:
- Discuss the tally chart and bar graph above. Help your child read the data.
- Then help your child choose a topic for a simple data gathering activity.
- Your child may wish to collect data about favorite ice cream flavors.
- Talk with your child about how to ask questions in a survey. Use questions such as: Do you like strawberry, vanilla, or chocolate ice cream the most?
- Help your child label the chart and graph on p. 243 to show what data will be gathered.
- Help your child use tally marks to complete the tally chart as he or she collects data.
- Then help your child display the data from the tally chart on the graph.
- Encourage your child to color and display the graph.

	Tally	Total
_____		

Family Projects

Help your child use the number cards on p. 245 and the activity on this sheet for practice with place value concepts.

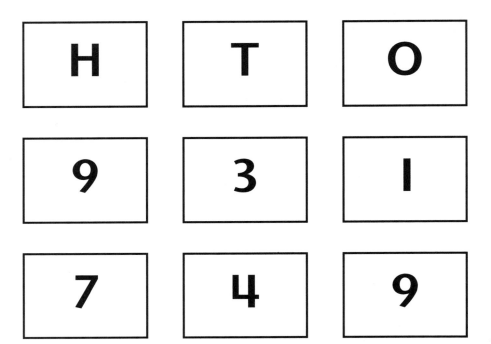

✂ –

Family Note:

- Make 3 sets of cards with the numbers 0–9 and a set with H, T, and O.
  Or duplicate page 245.
- The goal of the activity is to arrange digits to make the greatest possible number.
- Place the cards with H, T, and O, in a row.
- Tell your child that in this activity, H stands for hundreds, T for tens and O for ones.
- Explain to your child that each person selects a card from each of 3 sets of number cards and arranges them to make the greatest possible number.
- Help your child arrange the digits to make the greatest number possible.
- Ask your child to tell how many hundreds, tens, and ones are in his or her number.
- Have your child write the numbers on a separate sheet.
  Help your child compare the numbers. The player with the greater number wins the round.
  (You may wish to use the symbols > "is greater than" and < "is less than" to have your child compare the numbers.)
- Save the cards to use with the Unit 11 Family Project.

0	1	2	3
4	5	6	7
8	9	+	—
×	÷	>	<
H	T	O	

Family Projects

Use the cards from the Unit 10 Family Project to help your child practice adding and subtracting 3-digit numbers.

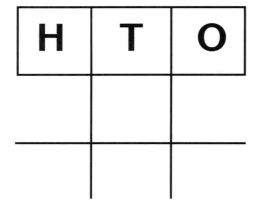
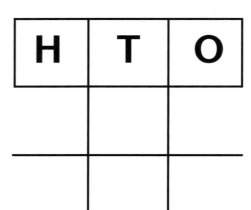
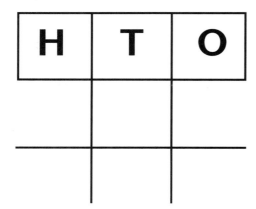
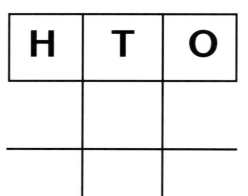

✂ -

Family Note:
- In this activity, you and your child take turns picking 3 number cards each.
- Each person arranges his or her cards to make a 3-digit number.
- Ask your child to select a + or − card.
- Help your child write each number in the spaces above, making either an addition or subtraction problem.
- If your child chooses a − card, remind him or her to write the greater number on top.
- Help your child solve the problem.
- Repeat several times.

Help your child use the graph paper on p. 248 and crayons to practice multiplication.

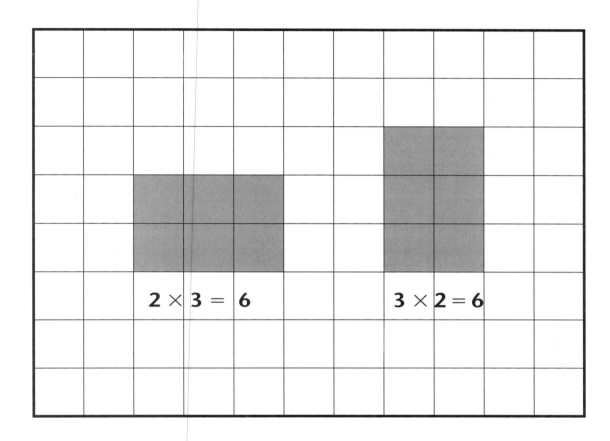

$2 \times 3 = 6$ $3 \times 2 = 6$

✂ –

Family Note:
- Discuss the arrays in the example above. Point out that 2×3 means 2 rows of 3 squares and 3×2 means 3 rows of 2 squares.
- Have your child count the number of squares in each array and compare with the products.
- Help your child make arrays to illustrate multiplication facts.
- Use the graph paper on page 248 and crayons.
- Have your child choose a fact and write it on the paper.
- Then ask him or her to draw an array to show the fact.
- Check to make sure the number of squares, or area, of the array matches the product.
- Repeat.
- When your child is finished, you may wish to display his or her arrays.

Family Projects

Answer
Keys

NOTES

Answer Key • Beginning of the Year Inventory

**Beginning of the Year Inventory,
pages 3–10**

1. 5
2. 4¢
3. 2; 2
4. 2; 2
5. 1
6. 3¢
7. $8 - 3 = 5$
8. $3 + 3 = 6$
9. $3 + 2 = 5$
   $2 + 3 = 5$
   $5 - 3 = 2$
   $5 - 2 = 3$
10. $6 + 1 = 7$
    $1 + 6 = 7$
    $7 - 6 = 1$
    $7 - 1 = 6$
11. 2 tens 2 ones = 22
12. 3 tens 2 ones = 32
13. 11
14. 12
15. 32
16 74
17. There should be a ring around the seventh flower.
18. 25, 26
19. 18, 16
20. 4
21. 3
22. 4
23. 3
24. 2
25. 3
26. Tuesday
27. Friday

28. 9
29. 9
30. 4:00
31. 9:30
32. 6
33. 10
34. 8
35. 8
36. 6
37. 7
38. 5
39. 8
40. 46
41. 52
42. 39
43. 75
44. 35¢
45. 32¢
46. 16, 18, 22
47. Children should color one fourth of the rectangle.
48. Children should color one third of the circle.
49. Children should ring the circle that is divided into equal parts.
50. Children should ring the pencil that is longer.
51. Children should ring the flower next to the tree and the bird above the flower.
52. rectangle
53. cone
54. three
55. four
56. Children should draw a triangle as the next shape in the pattern.
57. $3 + 4 = 7$
58. Check drawings; Kim
59. 20 crayons; Students should complete the chart.
60. 3; 3
61. no

Answer Key • Pretests and Posttests

Unit 1 Pretest, pages 11–12

1. 9; Possible answer: $9 - 3 = 6$
2. 9; Possible answer: $9 + 2 = 11$
3. 7; Possible answer: $7 - 3 = 4$
4.

4	5	9	9
+5	+4	−5	−4
9	9	4	5

5.

1	5	6	6
+5	+1	−5	−1
6	6	1	5

6.

3	9	12	12
+9	+3	−9	−3
12	12	3	9

7.

4	6	10	10
+6	+4	−6	−4
10	10	4	6

8. 9
9. 10
10. 8
11. 13
12. 11
13. 10
14. 8
15. 6
16. 2
17. 2
18. 8
19. 3
20. 7
21. 7
22. 2
23. 3
24. 5
25. 5
26. >
27. <
28. =
29. >
30. <
31. <
32. 6
33. 8
34. 14
35. 12
36. $4 + 8 = 12$; 12
37. $14 - 7 = 7$; 7

Unit 1 Posttest, pages 13–14

1. 6; Possible answer: $6 - 2 = 4$
2. 9; Possible answer: $9 + 3 = 12$

(Unit 1 Posttest, continued)

3. 13; Possible answer: $13 - 7 = 6$
4.

9	2	11	11
+2	+9	−2	−9
11	11	9	2

5.

3	5	8	8
+5	+3	−5	−3
8	8	3	5

6.

4	8	12	12
+8	+4	−8	−4
12	12	4	8

7.

6	3	9	9
+3	+6	−3	−6
9	9	6	3

8. 10
9. 12
10. 11
11. 10
12. 14
13. 8
14. 11
15. 6
16. 5
17. 6
18. 5
19. 2
20. 8
21. 8
22. 4
23. 6
24. 2
25. 4
26. <
27. >
28. =
29. >
30. =
31. <
32. 10
33. 9
34. 11
35. 13
36. $5 + 8 = 13$; 13
37. $9 - 5 = 4$; 4

Unit 2 Pretest, pages 15–16

1. 4, 3, 43
2. 6, 7, 67
3. <
4. >
5. >
6. =
7. <
8. >
9. <
10. >
11. 96

(Unit 2 Pretest, continued)

12. 16
13. 16
14. 35
15. 15
16. 12
17. 19
18. 21
19. 4, 7, 1, 8, 2, 5
20. 84, 51, 93
21. 40, 5, 45
22. 70, 2, 72
23. 16, 18, 20, 22, 26, 28, 30
24. 15, 20, 25, 30, 40, 45, 50
25. 5 dimes and 6 pennies to 56¢
26. 7 dimes and 1 penny to 71¢
27. 1 dime and 7 pennies to 17¢
28. Answers will vary; 34

Unit 2 Posttest, pages 17–18

1. 3, 2, 32
2. 5, 6, 56
3. >
4. <
5. <
6. =
7. <
8. =
9. <
10. >
11. 96
12. 44
13. 14
14. 31
15. 10
16. 16
17. 15
18. 20
19. 3, 6; 5, 8; 2, 9
20. 75, 53, 68
21. 30, 7, 37
22. 80, 0, 80
23. 6, 12, 15, 18, 24, 27, 30
24. 20, 30, 40, 50, 70, 80, 90, 100
25. 4 dimes and 9 pennies to 49¢
26. 6 dimes and 8 pennies to 68¢

(Unit 2 Posttest, continued)

27. 1 dime and 9 pennies to 19¢
28. Answers will vary; 33

Unit 3 Pretest, pages 19–20

1. 16; Possible answer: $16 - 7 = 9$
2. 7; Possible answer: $7 + 6 = 13$
3. 9; Possible answer: $9 + 8 = 17$
4.

5	9	14	14
+9	+5	−9	−5
14	14	5	9

5.

7	8	15	15
+8	+7	−8	−7
15	15	7	8

6.

8	16
+8	−8
16	8

7.

8	9	17	17
+9	+8	−9	−8
17	17	8	9

8. 6
9. 6
10. 8
11. 9
12. 9
13. 7
14. 5
15. +
16. −
17. +
18. −
19. >
20. <
21. =
22. <
23. <
24. >
25. 13
26. 17
27. 14
28. 17
29. $6 + 3 + 8 = 17$; 17
30. $13 - 8 = 5$; 5

Unit 3 Posttest, pages 21–22

1. 9; Possible answer: $9 + 9 = 18$
2. 7; Possible answer: $7 + 5 = 12$

Answer Key • Pretests and Posttests

(Unit 3 Posttest, continued)

3. 15; Possible answer:
$15 - 6 = 9$

4.
$$\begin{array}{cccc} 6 & 9 & 15 & 15 \\ +9 & +6 & -9 & -6 \\ \hline 15 & 15 & 6 & 9 \end{array}$$

5.
$$\begin{array}{cccc} 7 & 9 & 16 & 16 \\ +9 & +7 & -9 & -7 \\ \hline 16 & 16 & 7 & 9 \end{array}$$

6.
$$\begin{array}{cccc} 6 & 8 & 14 & 14 \\ +8 & +6 & -8 & -6 \\ \hline 14 & 14 & 6 & 8 \end{array}$$

7.
$$\begin{array}{cccc} 9 & 8 & 17 & 17 \\ +8 & +9 & -8 & -9 \\ \hline 17 & 17 & 9 & 8 \end{array}$$

8. 5
9. 6
10. 7
11. 8
12. 8
13. 8
14. 7
15. $+$
16. $-$
17. $+$
18. $-$
19. $<$
20. $=$
21. $>$
22. $<$
23. $=$
24. $=$
25. 16
26. 15
27. 18
28. 15
29. $5 + 6 + 2 = 13$; 13
30. $16 - 9 = 7$; 7

Unit 4 Pretest, pages 23–24

1. sphere to sphere
2. cone to cone
3. cube to cube
4. 6; yes; no
5. 5; no; no
6. 6; yes; no
7. 4; 4
8. 5; 5
9. 3; 3
10. (third figure)
11. one part shaded; $\frac{1}{5}$
12. one part shaded; $\frac{1}{8}$
13. one part shaded; $\frac{1}{12}$

(Unit 4 Pretest, continued)

14. one part shaded; $\frac{1}{9}$
15. $\frac{2}{5}$
16. $\frac{3}{4}$
17. $\frac{5}{6}$
18. $\frac{1}{8}$
19. 3
20. 2
21. 1, A
22. 2, C
23. 4, B

Unit 4 Posttest, pages 25–26

1. sphere to sphere
2. rectangular prism to rectangular prism
3. cylinder to cylinder
4. 2; yes; yes
5. 5; no; no
6. 1; no, yes
7. 4; 4
8. 6; 6
9. 0; 0
10. (fourth figure)
11. one part shaded; $\frac{1}{8}$
12. one part shaded; $\frac{1}{6}$
13. one part shaded; $\frac{1}{9}$
14. one part shaded; $\frac{1}{12}$
15. $\frac{4}{5}$
16. $\frac{3}{6}$
17. $\frac{3}{4}$
18. $\frac{4}{10}$
19. 12
20. 9
21. 4, B
22. 2, C
23. 1, A

Unit 5 Pretest, pages 27–28

1. 8 centimeters
2. 3 centimeters
3. 2 inches

(Unit 5 Pretest, continued)

4. 3 inches
5. less than a pound
6. more than a pound
7. more than a kilogram
8. less than a kilogram
9. about 2 inches
10. about 5 inches
11. 70 degrees
12. 20 degrees
13. 60 degrees
14. $2 + 1 + 2 + 2 = 7$; 7

Unit 5 Posttest, pages 29–30

1. 4 centimeters
2. 7 centimeters
3. 3 inches
4. 2 inches
5. more than a pound
6. less than a pound
7. less than a kilogram
8. more than a kilogram
9. about 5 inches
10. about 7 inches
11. 10 degrees
12. 30 degrees
13. 80 degrees
14. $3 + 2 + 2 = 7$; 7

Unit 6 Pretest, page 31

1. 5; 50
2. 7; 70
3. 45
4. 75
5. 47
6. 45
7. 69
8. 83
9. 53
10. 68¢
11. 64
12. 82¢
13. 79
14. 66
15. 77
16. 68
17. 50
18. 87
19. 76
20. 61
21. 88
22. 86
23. not enough information
24. 52 bananas

Unit 6 Posttest, page 32

1. 8; 80
2. 7; 70
3. 40
4. 85
5. 67
6. 61
7. 66
8. 60¢
9. 81
10. 79
11. 73
12. 72¢
13. 82
14. 80
15. 79
16. 89
17. 53
18. 90
19. 70
20. 89
21. 59
22. 77
23. not enough information
24. 70 ribbons

Unit 7 Pretest, page 33

1. 5; 50
2. 3; 30
3. 30
4. 45
5. 27
6. 39
7. 41
8. 33¢
9. 28
10. 20
11. 53
12. 22¢
13. 49
14. 11
15. 51
16. 2
17. 13
18. 23
19. 26
20. 65
21. 25¢
22. 19
23. 66
24. 12

Answer Key • Pretests and Posttests

Unit 7 Posttest, page 34

1. 1; 10
2. 3; 30
3. 35
4. 45
5. 27
6. 39
7. 50¢
8. 23
9. 39
10. 28
11. 42
12. 18
13. 51
14. 19
15. 11¢
16. 30
17. 19
18. 25¢
19. 27
20. 45
21. 21
22. 26
23. 15
24. 76

Unit 8 Pretest, pages 35–36

1.
2.
3.
4.
5. 60
6. 1
7. hours
8. 12
9. 4:15; 5:00; 45
10. 7:30; 9:30; 2
11. 36¢
12. 40¢
13. 50¢

(Unit 8 Pretest, continued)

14. 1 quarter, 1 dime, 2 pennies; or 1 quarter, 2 nickles, 2 pennies
15. 1 quarter, 1 dime, 2 nickels
16. 40¢, 30¢; >
17. 50¢, 50¢; =
18. 3 ways; 5 nickels; 3 nickels, 1 dime; 1 nickel, 2 dimes

Unit 8 Posttest, pages 37–38

1.
2.
3.
4.
5. 1
6. 7
7. 24
8. year
9. 6:30; 7:10; 40
10. 2:15; 4:15; 2
11. 32¢
12. 45¢
13. 36¢
14. 1 quarter, 1 nickel, 2 pennies; or 2 dimes, 2 nickels, 2 pennies
15. 1 quarter, 1 dime, 2 nickels, 3 pennies; or 1 quarter, 2 dimes, 3 pennies
16. 50¢, 35¢; >
17. 25¢, 40¢; <
18. 4 ways; 3 dimes, 1 nickel; 2 dimes, 3 nickels; 1 dime, 5 nickels; 7 nickles

Unit 9 Pretest, pages 37–38

1.

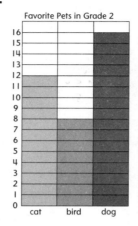

Favorite Pets in Grade 2

2. 12
3. bird
4. sometimes
5. more likely
6. 8 − 3 = 5; 5

Unit 9 Posttest, page 40

1.

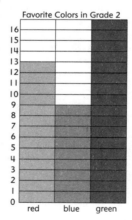

Favorite Colors in Grade 2

2. 9
3. green
4. never
5. less likely
6. 6 − 2 = 4; 4

Unit 10 Pretest, page 41

1. 339
2. 530
3. 420
4. 673

(Unit 10 Pretest, continued)

5. 718
6. 2; 0; 9
7. 6; 6; 8
8. 471
9. 543
10. 707
11. 960
12. 70¢; $.70
13. 46¢; $.46
14. 75¢ > $.65; dog

Unit 10 Posttest, page 42

1. 289
2. 620
3. 681
4. 641
5. 389
6. 7; 7; 2
7. 5; 0; 6
8. 907
9. 482
10. 630
11. 819
12. 76¢; $.76
13. 47¢; $.47
14. $.70 > 50¢; bird

Unit 11 Pretest, page 43

1. 592
2. 309
3. 421
4. 694
5. 342
6. 999
7. 585
8. 469
9. 595
10. 529
11. 582
12. 724
13. 788
14. 256
15. 890
16. $3.80
17. $5.09
18. $6.54
19. $2.13
20. $4.25
21. $3.96
22. $2.48

Answer Key • Pretests and Posttests

Unit 11 Posttest, page 44

1. 138
2. 206
3. 673
4. 663
5. 214
6. 881
7. 409
8. 728
9. 690
10. 129
11. 791
12. 512
13. 664
14. 469
15. 593
16. $3.80
17. $5.19
18. $6.83
19. $2.36
20. $4.48
21. $4.77
22. $2.77

Unit 12 Pretest, pages 45–46

1. 2, 4, 6, 8, 10; 5; 2; 10
2. 3, 6, 9, 12; 4; 3; 12
3. 5, 10, 15; 3; 5; 15
4. 8
5. 18
6. 14
7. 12
8. 15
9. 4
10. 50
11. 12
12. 24
13. 20
14. 10
15. 0
16. 18
17. 25
18. 60
19. 20
20. 21
21. 90
22. 9
23. 8
24. 3
25. 5
26. 3
27. 2
28. 2
29. 5

(Unit 12 Pretest, continued)

30. multiply; $8 \times 2 = 16$; 16; or add; $2 + 2 + 2 + 2 + 2 + 2 + 2 + 2 = 16$; 16

Unit 12 Posttest, pages 47–48

1. 5, 10, 15; 3; 5; 15
2. 2, 4, 6, 8, 10; 5; 2; 10
3. 3, 6, 9, 12; 4; 3; 12
4. 8
5. 12
6. 10
7. 6
8. 12
9. 30
10. 14
11. 27
12. 16
13. 40
14. 18
15. 3
16. 0
17. 20
18. 4
19. 15
20. 0
21. 12
22. 24
23. 80
24. 3
25. 5
26. 5
27. 3
28. 4
29. 3
30. multiply; $2 \times 8 = 16$ legs; 16; or add; $8 + 8 = 16$; 16

Answer Key • Midyear Test and Final Test

Midyear Test, pages 51–56

1. second choice, $14 - 8 = 6$
2. fourth choice, 13
3. third choice, 60
4. third choice, 9
5. third choice, 40
6. third choice, 50
7. third choice, 68
8. first choice, 5 dimes
9. fourth choice, $6 + 8 = 14$
10. first choice, $16 - 9 = 7$
11. second choice, $15 - 7 = 8$
12. first choice, cylinder
13. second choice, pentagon
14. fourth choice, $\frac{1}{12}$
15. third choice, $\frac{3}{8}$
16. fourth choice, $\frac{5}{9}$
17. first choice, 12 baseballs with 6 shaded
18. first choice: 3, B
19. fourth choice, 5 inches
20. third choice, 10 centimeters
21. fourth choice, dictionary
22. first choice, shows 30 degrees
23. second choice, 7 pounds
24. fourth choice, 28, 36
25. second choice, 7
26. third choice, >
27. fifth choice, NH
28. second choice, 8
29. third choice, 9
30. fifth choice, NH
31. second choice, 67
32. fifth choice, NH

Final Test, pages 59–66

1. third choice, 57
2. third choice, shows $\frac{1}{4}$ shaded
3. third choice, 5 inches
4. second choice, 70
5. fourth choice, $\begin{array}{r} 80 \\ -\ 30 \\ \hline 50 \end{array}$
6. first choice, clock shows 8:55
7. second choice, clock shows 7:25
8. fourth choice, 4 hours
9. third choice, 47¢
10. third choice, worth 56¢
11. third choice, art class
12. third choice, 3:00
13. first choice, 3
14. fourth choice, 9
15. first choice, white marble
16. third choice, $20 - 10 = 10$
17. third choice, 796
18. second choice, 374
19. fourth choice, $900 + 40 + 7$
20. first choice, $1.27
21. fourth choice, 100
22. fourth choice, 100
23. second choice, $4 \times 4 = 16$
24. third choice, 6
25. first choice, shows 4 plates with 5 strawberries on each
26. third choice, 11
27. second choice, 9
28. third choice, 76
29. fifth choice, NH
30. third choice, 50
31. second choice, 64
32. third choice, 31
33. first choice, 47
34. second choice, 691
35. fifth choice, NH
36. fifth choice, NH
37. third choice, $7.81
38. third choice, 30
39. fourth choice, 70

Answer Key • Reteach Worksheets

Reteach 1, page 69

1. 8; 8
2. 8; 8
3. 7; 2; 7
4. 7; 3; 7
5. 10; 3 + 7 = 10
6. 5; 0 + 5 = 5

Reteach 2, page 70

1.
```
  3    9
 +6   −6
  9    3
```
2.
```
  5    6
 +1   −1
  6    5
```
3.
```
  3    8
 +5   −5
  8    3
```
4.
```
 10    9
 −1   +1
  9   10
```
5.
```
  9    4
 −5   +5
  4    9
```
6.
```
  6    4
 −2   +2
  4    6
```

Reteach 3, page 71

1. 6; 2; 4
2. 10; 10; 4; 6
3. 4; 4; 3; 1
4.
```
  7    3   10   10
 +3   +7   −3   −7
 10   10    7    3
```
5.
```
  5    3    8    8
 +3   +5   −3   −5
  8    8    5    3
```
6.
```
  1    7    8    8
 +7   +1   −7   −1
  8    8    1    7
```

Reteach 4, page 72

1. 4
2. 1
3. 2
4. 5
5. 3
6. 5
7. 2
8. 5
9. 1
10. 3
11. 0
12. 1

Reteach 5, page 73

1.
```
  6   11
 +5   −5
 11    6
```
2.
```
  8   13
 +5   −5
 13    8
```
3.
```
  6   12
 +6   −6
 12    6
```
4.
```
 14    9
 −5   +5
  9   14
```
5.
```
 11    4
 −7   +7
  4   11
```
6.
```
 12    4
 −8   +8
  4   12
```

Reteach 6, page 74

1. 11; 9; 2
2. 13; 13; 8; 5
3. 12; 12; 5; 7
4.
```
  8    4
 +4   +8
 12   12

 12   12
 −4   −8
  8    4
```
5.
```
  9    5
 +5   +9
 14   14

 14   14
 −5   −9
  9    5
```
6.
```
  3    8
 +8   +3
 11   11

 11   11
 −8   −3
  3    8
```

Reteach 7, page 75

1. 12; 6; 12
   12; 10; 12
2. 14; 8; 14
   14; 7; 14
3. 11
4. 13
5. 12
6. 12

Reteach 8, page 76

1. 3; 4; 5; 6; 7
2. 2; 3; 4; 5; 6
3. 1; 2; 3; 4; 5

(Reteach 8, continued)

4. 10; 5
5. 10; 4
6. 10; 3

Reteach 9, page 77

1. =; ≠; =
2. ≠; =; =
3. = ; ≠; ≠
4. ≠; =; =
5. =; ≠; =
6. ≠; = ; ≠
7. ≠; =; =
8. ≠; =; ≠
9. =; ≠; =

Reteach 10, page 78

1. <
2. >
3. >
4. >; <; <; =
5. >; =; <; <
6. <; >; =; <

Reteach 11, page 79

1. 12; 11; 13
2. 13; 10; 9
3. 9; 8; 4
4. 14; 10; 11
5. 10; 9; 8
6. 3; 5; 4

Reteach 12, page 80

1. 4; 43
   40; 43
2. 5; 5; 55
   50; 5; 55
3. 60; 2; 62
4. 90; 8; 98
5. 20; 6; 26
6. 4; 1
7. 9; 4
8. 3; 8
9. 1; 2
10. 24
11. 9

Reteach 13, page 81

1. 24; 27; 30; 31; 36; 39;
   44; 45; 47; 50; 51; 53; 56;
   58; 59
2. (ring; 25, 30, 35, 40, 45,
   50, 55, 60)
3. (red; 23, 33, 43, 53)
4. (blue; 40–49)
5. 63
   86
   19
   94

(Reteach 13, continued)

6. 34
   50
   21
   100
7. 95
   40
   91
   50

Reteach 14, page 82

1. 4; 6; 10; 12
2. 15; 20; 30
3. 20; 30; 60
4. 6; 9; 15; 18
5. 28; 30; 32
6. 75; 80; 85
7. 39; 42; 45
8. 80; 90; 100

Reteach 15, page 83

1. (20)
2. (50)
3. 60, 70, 70, 60, 60
4. 30, 20, 20, 30, 30

Reteach 16, page 84

1. 20
2. 50
3. 60¢
4. 80¢
5. 90¢
6. 40¢
7. 30¢
8. 70¢

Reteach 17, page 85

1. 52¢
2. 3; 5; 35¢
3. 2; 1; 21¢
4. 46¢
5. 68¢
6. 27¢

Reteach 18, page 86

1.
```
  3   11
 +8   −8
 11    3
```
2.
```
  7   15
 +8   −8
 15    7
```

Answer Key • Reteach Worksheets

(Reteach 18, continued)

3. $\begin{array}{r} 9 \\ +6 \\ \hline 15 \end{array}$ $\begin{array}{r} 15 \\ -6 \\ \hline 9 \end{array}$

4. $\begin{array}{r} 12 \\ -5 \\ \hline 7 \end{array}$ $\begin{array}{r} 7 \\ +5 \\ \hline 12 \end{array}$

5. $\begin{array}{r} 13 \\ -5 \\ \hline 8 \end{array}$ $\begin{array}{r} 8 \\ +5 \\ \hline 13 \end{array}$

6. $\begin{array}{r} 16 \\ -8 \\ \hline 8 \end{array}$ $\begin{array}{r} 8 \\ +8 \\ \hline 16 \end{array}$

7. 11; 11 − 4 = 7
8. 13; Possible answer: 13 − 4 = 9
9. 7; Possible answer: 7 + 6 = 13

Reteach 19, page 87

1. 14; 6; 8
2. 16; 16; 7; 9
3. 11; 11; 9; 2
4. $\begin{array}{r} 7 \\ +8 \\ \hline 15 \end{array}$ $\begin{array}{r} 8 \\ +7 \\ \hline 15 \end{array}$ $\begin{array}{r} 15 \\ -8 \\ \hline 7 \end{array}$ $\begin{array}{r} 15 \\ -7 \\ \hline 8 \end{array}$

5. $\begin{array}{r} 7 \\ +7 \\ \hline 14 \end{array}$ $\begin{array}{r} 14 \\ -7 \\ \hline 7 \end{array}$

6. $\begin{array}{r} 6 \\ +7 \\ \hline 13 \end{array}$ $\begin{array}{r} 7 \\ +6 \\ \hline 13 \end{array}$ $\begin{array}{r} 13 \\ -7 \\ \hline 6 \end{array}$ $\begin{array}{r} 13 \\ -6 \\ \hline 7 \end{array}$

Reteach 20, page 88

1. $\begin{array}{r} 9 \\ +9 \\ \hline 18 \end{array}$ $\begin{array}{r} 18 \\ -9 \\ \hline 9 \end{array}$

2. $\begin{array}{r} 9 \\ +8 \\ \hline 17 \end{array}$ $\begin{array}{r} 17 \\ -8 \\ \hline 9 \end{array}$

3. $\begin{array}{r} 8 \\ +8 \\ \hline 16 \end{array}$ $\begin{array}{r} 16 \\ -8 \\ \hline 8 \end{array}$

4. 13; 13 − 5 = 8
5. 15; Possible answer: 15 − 6 = 9
6. 9; Possible answer: 9 + 5 = 14
7. $\begin{array}{r} 4 \\ +7 \\ \hline 11 \end{array}$ $\begin{array}{r} 11 \\ -7 \\ \hline 4 \end{array}$

8. $\begin{array}{r} 17 \\ -8 \\ \hline 9 \end{array}$ $\begin{array}{r} 9 \\ +8 \\ \hline 17 \end{array}$

9. $\begin{array}{r} 12 \\ -9 \\ \hline 3 \end{array}$ $\begin{array}{r} 3 \\ +9 \\ \hline 12 \end{array}$

Reteach 21, page 89

1. 15; 7; 8
2. 11; 11; 9; 2
3. $\begin{array}{r} 4 \\ +8 \\ \hline 12 \end{array}$ $\begin{array}{r} 8 \\ +4 \\ \hline 12 \end{array}$ $\begin{array}{r} 12 \\ -8 \\ \hline 4 \end{array}$ $\begin{array}{r} 12 \\ -4 \\ \hline 8 \end{array}$

4. $\begin{array}{r} 9 \\ +9 \\ \hline 18 \end{array}$ $\begin{array}{r} 18 \\ -9 \\ \hline 9 \end{array}$

5. $\begin{array}{r} 7 \\ +7 \\ \hline 14 \end{array}$ $\begin{array}{r} 14 \\ -7 \\ \hline 9 \end{array}$

6. $\begin{array}{r} 6 \\ +7 \\ \hline 13 \end{array}$ $\begin{array}{r} 7 \\ +6 \\ \hline 13 \end{array}$ $\begin{array}{r} 13 \\ -7 \\ \hline 6 \end{array}$ $\begin{array}{r} 13 \\ -6 \\ \hline 7 \end{array}$

Reteach 22, page 90

1. 14; 13; 15
2. 7; 8; 9
3. 7; 5; 4
4. 13; 15; 17
5. 9; 8; 4
6. 9; 7; 6

Reteach 23, page 91

1. 17; 17
   10; 10
2. 16; 10
3. 15; 10
4. 14; 10
5. 13; 10

Reteach 24, page 92

1. 0; 2; 0; yes; yes
2. 8; 6; 12; yes; no
3. 0; 1; 1; no; yes
4. 5; 5; 8; no; no

Reteach 25, page 93

1. (circle), circle
2. (triangle), triangle
3. (square), square
4. (circle), circle
5. (rectangle), rectangle
6. (triangle or rectangle), triangle or rectangle

Reteach 26, page 94

1. s; s; yes
2. s; d; no
3. d; s; no

(Reteach 26, continued)

4. s; s; yes
5. bat; ring

Reteach 27, page 95

1. one part shaded; $\frac{1}{2}$
2. one part shaded; $\frac{1}{3}$
3. one part shaded; $\frac{1}{4}$
4. $\frac{1}{4}$
5. $\frac{1}{2}$
6. $\frac{1}{3}$

Reteach 28, page 96

1. $\frac{3}{4}$
2. $\frac{2}{3}$
3. $\frac{3}{6}$
4. $\frac{4}{8}$
5. $\frac{2}{5}$
6. $\frac{3}{8}$

Reteach 29, page 97

1. 2
2. 4
3. 2
4. 4
5. 1
6. 2

Reteach 30, page 98

1. 8; 7
2. Answers will vary; 6
3. Check children's work.
4. Check children's work.

Reteach 31, page 99

1. 5
2. 3
3. Check children's work.
4. Check children's work.

Reteach 32, page 100

1. 15; 14
2. 5; 5
3. Check children's work.
4. Check children's work.

Reteach 33, page 101

1. about 1 pound
2. more than 1 pound
3. less than 1 pound
4. about 1 pound

Reteach 34, page 102

1. about 1 kilogram
2. less than 1 kilogram
3. about 1 kilogram
4. more than 1 kilogram

Reteach 35, page 103

1. 3
2. 6
3. 2
4. 3
5. 2; 2
6. 4; 2

Reteach 36, page 104

1. about 1 liter
2. more than 1 liter
3. less than 1 liter
4. less than 1 liter
5. about 1 liter
6. more than 1 liter

Reteach 37, page 105

1. 20
2. 70
3. 30

Reteach 38, page 106

1. 42
2. 53
3. 62
4. 31
5. 72
6. 25
7. 42
8. 50

Reteach 39, page 107

1. 50
2. 81
3. 82

Answer Key • Reteach Worksheets

(Reteach 39, continued)
4. 40
5. 60
6. 91
7. 92
8. 71

Reteach 40, page 108
1. 43
2. 64
3. 54
4. 34
5. 24
6. 73
7. 63
8. 84

Reteach 41, page 109
1. 54
2. 84
3. 93
4. 53
5. 84
6. 93
7. 93
8. 33

Reteach 42, page 110
1. 45
2. 76
3. 82
4. 35
5. 65
6. 86
7. 76
8. 96

Reteach 43, page 111
1. 68¢
2. 90¢
3. 94¢
4. 73¢
5. 92¢
6. 70¢
7. 72¢
8. 57¢

Reteach 44, page 112
1. 76
2. 65
3. 83
4. 87
5. 79
6. 94
7. 98
8. 82

Reteach 45, page 113
1. 43
2. 66
3. 22
4. 18
5. 36
6. 45
7. 54
8. 73

Reteach 46, page 114
1. 33
2. 66
3. 25
4. 34
5. 42
6. 26
7. 24
8. 18

Reteach 47, page 115
1. 35
2. 62
3. 54
4. 36
5. 43
6. 11
7. 37
8. 8

Reteach 48, page 116
1. 33¢
2. 64¢
3. 37¢
4. 25¢
5. 35¢
6. 63¢

Reteach 49, page 117
1. 76
2. 67
3. 24
4. 19
5. 38
6. 47
7. 56
8. 75

Reteach 50, page 118
1. 38
2. 67
3. 47
4. 55
5. 44

(Reteach 50, continued)
6. 29
7. 25
8. 17

Reteach 51, page 119
1. 39
2. 38
3. 28
4. 37
5. 27
6. 37
7. 19
8. 19

Reteach 52, page 120
1. 24; 53

2. 29;   29
         $+19$
         48

3. 48;   48
         $+29$
         77

4. 19;   19
         $+31$
         50

5. 17;   17
         $+45$
         62

6. 17;   17
         $+67$
         84

Reteach 53, page 121
1.   42
    $+29$
     71

2.   61
    -15
     46

3.   56
    $+28$
     84

4.   38
    $+47$
     85

(Reteach 53, continued)
5.   70
    -43
     27

6.   83
    -19
     64

7.   40
    -16
     24

8.   58
    $+39$
     97

9.   22
    $+28$
     50

Reteach 54, page 122
1. 8:00
2. 10:00
3. 6:00
4. 2 o'clock
5. 5 o'clock
6. 11 o'clock

Reteach 55, page 123
1. 4:30
2. 12:30
3. 9:30
4. half past 3
5. half past 7
6. half past 1

Reteach 56, page 124
1. 6:15
2. 2:15
3. 8:15
4. quarter past 5
5. quarter past 10
6. quarter past 12

Reteach 57, page 125
1. 2:45
2. 11:45
3. 7:45
4. quarter to 7
5. quarter to 10
6. quarter to 3

Reteach 58, page 126
1. 10
2. 20

Answer Key • Reteach Worksheets

(Reteach 58, continued)
3. 50
4. 35
5. 25
6. 40

Reteach 59, page 127
1. 3
2. 2
3. 1

Reteach 60, page 128
1. May
2. 31
3. 7
4. Thursday

Reteach 61, page 129
1. 5¢, 10¢, 15¢; 15¢
2. 10¢, 20¢, 30¢; 30¢
3. 10¢, 15¢; 15¢

Reteach 62, page 130
1. 10¢, 20¢, 25¢, 26¢; 26¢
2. 10¢, 15¢, 20¢, 21¢; 21¢
3. 10¢, 11¢, 12¢,13¢; 13¢

Reteach 63, page 131
1. 25¢, 30¢; 30¢
2. 25¢, 35¢; 35¢
3. 25¢, 35¢, 36¢;36¢

Reteach 64, page 132
1. 27¢; yes
2. 46¢; no
3. 44¢; no
4. 32¢; yes

Reteach 65, page 133
1. 31¢;   35¢
         −31¢
           4¢

2. 44¢;   45¢
         −44¢
           1¢

Reteach 66, page 134
1. 3 tally marks; 3
2. 4 tally marks; 4
3. 4 tally marks; 4
4. 1 tally mark; 1

Reteach 67, page 135
1. 2 tally marks; 2
2. 3 tally marks; 3
3. 4 tally marks; 4
4. biking
5. skating

Reteach 68, page 136
1. Book Club: 6; Bike Club: 10; Computer Club: 5
2. 6
3. 5

Reteach 69, page 137
1. greatest
2. mode
3. greatest
4. least
5. six
6. range

Reteach 70, page 138
1. sometimes
2. never
3. sometimes
4. always

Reteach 71, page 139
1. 101
2. 102
3. 103
4. 104
5. 105
6. 106
7. 107
8. 108
9. 109

Reteach 72, page 140
1. 111, 112, 114, 115, 116, 117, 118, 120
2. 138, 139, 140, 141, 142, 144, 145, 146
3. 158, 159, 160, 162, 163, 164, 165, 166
4. 169, 171, 172, 173, 174, 175, 177, 178
5. 118, 119, 120, 122, 123, 124, 126, 127
6. 127, 129, 130, 131, 132, 134, 135, 136
7. 191, 192, 194, 195, 196, 197, 198, 200
8. 180, 181, 182, 183, 185, 186, 187, 188

Reteach 73, page 141
1. 2, 8, 0; 200, 80, 0; 280
2. 2, 0, 8; 200, 0, 8; 208
3. 2, 4, 3; 200; 40; 3; 243

Reteach 74, page 142
1. 3, 1, 5; 300, 10, 5; 315
2. 3, 0, 8, 300, 0, 8; 308
3. 3, 5, 3, 300, 50, 3; 353

Reteach 75, page 143
1. 4, 1, 8; 400, 10, 8; 418
2. 4, 0, 7; 400, 0, 7; 407
3. 4, 7, 3; 400, 70, 3; 473

Reteach 76, page 144
1. 28¢; $.28
2. 37¢; $.37
3. 40¢; $.40
4. 75¢; $.75

Reteach 77, page 145
1. $2.00
2. $4.00
3. $1.40
4. $3.50
5. $1.20
6. $7.50

Reteach 78, page 146
1. 1, 0, 3; $1.03
2. $8.10
3. $4.09
4. $1.69
5. $5.87
6. $9.10

Reteach 79, page 147
1. $.50
2. $.50
3. $1.00
4. $1.00

Reteach 80, page 148
1. 239
2. 132
3. 235
4. 738
5. 248
6. 361
7. 970
8. 829
9. 191
10. 563
11. 789

(Reteach 80, continued)
12. 292
13. 638
14. 179

Reteach 81, page 149
1. 213
2. 699
3. 405
4. 376
5. 888
6. 112
7. 593
8. 100
9. 998
10. 722
11. 867
12. 401
13. 525

Reteach 82, page 150
1. 880
2. 790
3. 386
4. 487
5. 781
6. 585
7. 680
8. 891

Reteach 83, page 151
1. 309
2. 319
3. 516
4. 209
5. 626
6. 229
7. 439
8. 238

Reteach 84, page 152
1. $4.73
2. $7.10
3. $8.39
4. $7.59
5. $9.59
6. $6.87
7. $4.75
8. $6.99
9. $2.32
10. $2.00
11. $2.10
12. $7.01
13. $.13
14. $2.54
15. $4.44
16. $4.53

Answer Key • Reteach Worksheets

Reteach 85, page 153

1. 4
2. 10
3. 6

Reteach 86, page 154

1. $2 + 2 + 2 + 2 = 8$
2. $2 + 2 + 2 = 6$
3. $2 + 2 + 2 + 2 + 2 = 10$

Reteach 87, page 155

1. 2; 2; 4; 4
2. 4; 2; 8; 8
3. 6; 2; 12; 12
4. 5; 2; 10; 10

Reteach 88, page 156

1. 6
2. 9
3. 12
4. 15
5. 18
6. 21
7. 24
8. 27

Reteach 89, page 157

1. 15
2. 25
3. 25
4. 30
5. 35
6. 40
7. 45

Reteach 90, page 158

1. $1 \times 5 = 5$;
   $5 \times 1 = 5$
2. $3 \times 4 = 12$;
   $4 \times 3 = 12$
3. $5 \times 3 = 15$;
   $3 \times 5 = 15$

Reteach 91, page 159

1. $5 \times 10 = 50$
2. $7 \times 10 = 70$
3. 60
4. 0
5. 90
6. 10
7. 80

Reteach 92, page 160

1. 6; 8; 10; 12; 14;
   16; 18; 20
2. 15; 20; 25; 30;
   35; 40; 45; 50
3. 30; 40; 50; 60;
   70; 80; 90; 100

Reteach 93, page 161

1. 5; 10
2. 4; 8
3. lion
4. 2

Reteach 94, page 162

1. 2
2. 3
3. 4
4. 3

Reteach 95, page 163

1. 8; ring 2 groups
   of 4; 4
2. 9; ring 3 groups
   of 3; 3
3. 10; ring 5 groups
   of 2; 2

Reteach 96, page 164

1. 10; 8; 6; 4; 2; 0; 6; 6
2. 12; 9; 6; 3; 0; 5; 5

Reteach 97, page 165

1. 9; ring 4 groups
   of 2; 4; 1
2. 11; ring 3 groups
   of 3; 3; 2
3. 15; ring 3 groups
   of 4; 3; 3

Answer Key • Extension Worksheets

Extension 1, page 169

(Check children's work.)

Extension 2, page 170

1. $+4$
2. $+3$
3. -7
4. -6
5. $+5$

Extension 3, page 171

1. 50, 80, 30, 100
2. 30, 60, 90, 20
3. 20, 80, 70, 40
4. 20, 20, 30, 80

Extension 4, page 172

1. 16; 22
2. 36
3. 17; 25
4. 54; 66
5. 70; 60

Extension 5, page 173

Puzzle 1: (Check children's work.)

Puzzle 2: $9 - 5 + 3 = 7$;
$9 + 5 + 3 = 17$
$9 + 2 - 6 = 5$;
$9 - 2 - 6 = 1$

Puzzle 3: $8 - 4 + 7 = 11$;
$8 + 4 - 7 = 5$
$8 - 3 - 5 = 0$;
$8 + 3 - 5 = 6$

Puzzle 4: (Check children's work.)

Extension 6, page 174

1. (first figure),
   (third figure),
   (fourth figure)
2. open
3. open
4. closed
5. open

Extension 7, page 175

1. true
2. false
3. false
4. true

(Extension 7, continued)

5. true
6. false
7. $<$
8. $=$
9. $<$

Extension 8, page 176

1. 8 paper clips
2. 2 markers
3. 3 markers
4. 5 erasers
5. 4 quarters

Extension 9, page 177

1. 8 square units
2. 9 square units
3. (Children should color 9 square units.)
4. (Children should color 12 square units.)

Extension 10, page 178

1.
$$\begin{array}{r} 20; 60 \\ + 40 \\ \hline 60 \end{array}$$

2.
$$\begin{array}{r} 60; 90 \\ + 30 \\ \hline 90 \end{array}$$

3.
$$\begin{array}{r} 30; 90 \\ 30 \\ + 30 \\ \hline 90 \end{array}$$

Extension 11, page 179

13, 16, 17, 31, 36, 37
61, 63, 67, 71, 73, 76

1. 76
2. 13
3. $76 + 13 = 89$
4. (Check children's work.)
5. (Check children's work.)
6. (Check children's work.)
7. (Check children's work.)

Extension 12, page 180

1.
$$\begin{array}{r} 23 \\ + 45 \\ \hline 68 \end{array}$$
2.
$$\begin{array}{r} 47 \\ + 22 \\ \hline 69 \end{array}$$

3.
$$\begin{array}{r} 62 \\ + 33 \\ \hline 95 \end{array}$$
4.
$$\begin{array}{r} 45 \\ + 43 \\ \hline 88 \end{array}$$

(Extension 12, continued)

5.
$$\begin{array}{r} 33 \\ + 42 \\ \hline 75 \end{array}$$
6.
$$\begin{array}{r} 72 \\ + 24 \\ \hline 96 \end{array}$$

Extension 13, page 181

1.
$$\begin{array}{r} 40; 10 \\ - 30 \\ \hline 10 \end{array}$$

2.
$$\begin{array}{r} 60; 40 \\ - 20 \\ \hline 40 \end{array}$$

3. about 30
4. about 30¢

Extension 14, page 182

(Check children's work.)

Extension 15, page 183

1. 22 fish;
$$\begin{array}{r} 27 \\ -13; \\ \hline 14 \end{array} \begin{array}{r} 14 \\ +8 \\ \hline 22 \end{array}$$

2. 49 fish;
$$\begin{array}{r} 15 \\ 21 \\ +27; \\ \hline 63 \end{array} \begin{array}{r} 63 \\ -14 \\ \hline 49 \end{array}$$

3. 15¢; Yes;
$$\begin{array}{r} 15¢ \\ 27¢ \\ +42¢; \\ \hline 84¢ \end{array} \begin{array}{r} 99¢ \\ -84¢ \\ \hline 15¢ \end{array}$$

Extension 16, page 184

(Check children's work.)

1. 4 hours
2. 1:00 P.M.
3. 11:30 A.M.
4. 12:00 P.M.

Extension 17, page 185

1. 3 weeks
2. 27 days
3. 2 minutes
4. 300 seconds
5. 30 hours
6. 2 days
7. 2 hours
8. 3 hours
9. 50 hours is longer than 2 days because 2 days equals 48 hours; $50 > 48$.

Extension 18, page 186

(Check children's work.)

Extension 19, page 187

(Check children's work.)

Extension 20, page 188

1. Three of the four sections are gray, so you are more likely to stop on gray.
2. 1 chance in 5
3. 1 chance in 5
4. 3 chances in 5
5. Three of the five sections are gray, so you are more likely to stop on gray.
6. You will not stop on red because there are no red sections on this spinner.

Extension 21, page 189

1. 132 pennies
2. 212 pennies
3. 18 dimes
4. 35 dimes
5. 27 nickels
6. 72 nickels
7. 16 quarters
8. 26 quarters

Extension 22, page 190

1. $1 + 3 + 7 = 11$
2. $2 + 8 + 1 = 11$
3. $3 + 4 + 6 = 13$
4. $4 + 6 + 7 = 17$
5. $5 + 4 + 4 = 13$
6. $8 + 9 + 2 = 19$
7. Check children's work. Possible answers: 486; 396.

Extension 23, page 191

1. 9; 27, 36, 45; 63; 81
2. 9
3. 9
4. 9
5. The sum of the digits is each equal to 9.
7. 25; 50; 75; 100 125; 150; 175; 200; 225; 250; 275; 300; 325; 350; 375; 400; 425; 450; 475; 500

Answer Key • Extension Worksheets

Extension 24, page 192

1. $2 \times 1 = 2$
   $2 \times 2 = 4$
   $2 \times 3 = 6$
   $2 \times 4 = 8$
   $2 \times 5 = 10$
   $2 \times 6 = 12$
   $2 \times 7 = 14$
   $2 \times 8 = 16$
   $2 \times 9 = 18$
   $2 \times 10 = 20$

2. $5 \times 1 = 5$
   $5 \times 2 = 10$
   $5 \times 3 = 15$
   $5 \times 4 = 20$
   $5 \times 5 = 25$
   $5 \times 6 = 30$
   $5 \times 7 = 35$
   $5 \times 8 = 40$
   $5 \times 9 = 45$
   $5 \times 10 = 50$

3. $10 \times 1 = 10$
   $10 \times 2 = 20$
   $10 \times 3 = 30$
   $10 \times 4 = 40$
   $10 \times 5 = 50$
   $10 \times 6 = 60$
   $10 \times 7 = 70$
   $10 \times 8 = 80$
   $10 \times 9 = 90$
   $10 \times 10 = 100$

4. THE TEMPERATURE

Extension 25, page 193

1. 10 rows; $3 \times 10 = 30$
2. 6 rows; $5 \times 6 = 30$